Rambling Sandlings

The thoughtful walker's guide to East Suffolk

SHIONA HARDIE

Illustrated by Janice Murray

BEULAH SHEEP

Sandscape Publishing

Published by Sandscape Publishing
18 Tennyson Close, Woodbridge, Suffolk IP12 4LB
© Sandscape Publishing 1995
ISBN 0 9526087 0 7

The rights of way described in the book were correct, to the best of the author's knowledge, at the time of writing. Neither the author nor the Publisher can accept responsibility for damage, trespass or nuisance caused by others in the course of negotiating the walks herein described or for errors due to the re-routing or closing of footpaths, or misunderstood directions.

A CIP catalogue record for this book is available from the British Library.

Author's Acknowledgements
Many thanks to Helen, Bruce, Ann, Colin, Janice and Pilly, who allowed themselves to be bullied, bribed, or otherwise coerced into undertaking some of these walks – with apparent enjoyment. I am also grateful to Charles Beardall and Mark Sly of the Suffolk Wildlife Trust for supplying the cover photographs. Thanks to Robert Markham, geologist at the Ipswich Museum, for information on the Sandlings surface geology. Thanks also to the various reserve wardens for many snippets of information. Last, but not least, thanks are due to Lindsey Freeman and Hally Hardie for checking details, and to Hally for the original idea.

Edited by Giala Murray
Designed by Mick Keates and Concise Artisans
Printed and bound by The Ipswich Book Company Ltd, Suffolk
Front cover photograph: C H Beardall/Suffolk Wildlife Trust
Back cover photograph: M Sly/Suffolk Wildlife Trust

CONTENTS

INTRODUCTION

THE SANDLINGS has been described as the area of East Suffolk from the Deben to the Alde, or from Ipswich to Lowestoft, or varying stretches in between these two. For the purposes of this book, however, the Sandlings specifies the area from the Blyth to the Orwell and from the coast to the A12.

The walks are arranged around the different river estuaries; the Blyth, Dunwich and Minsmere rivers; the Alde and Hundred rivers; the Ore, Butley and Deben area, and the Orwell/Deben peninsular. The walks vary in length and ease; whilst it is assumed that walkers have a car, it is possible, with planning, to do most of them using public transport – at least at some times of the year. One or two walks are also accessible to those who enjoy walking but find it difficult.

Each chapter contains a sketch map and instructions for the walk. Although the main idea is to describe the routes of the walks, it is assumed that many walkers will be interested to know something of the history of the landscape through which they are walking. The introductory chapters discuss in detail the formation of the area in general, its ecology and special features, and background information is also given at the beginning of each walk.

We also realise that walking in fresh air creates an appetite, so we've looked out for interesting pubs with good bar meals, cafés, and other eating places. Places of particular local interest are also noted. It is, for the most part, an unashamedly subjective list!

Every walk has been tried recently by the author and friends, and the eating places, if described, sampled. Whilst every effort has been made to provide accurate, up-to-date information, things can change and we cannot take responsibility for that.

MAPS

OS Landranger series, 156 Saxmundham and 169 Ipswich cover the Sandlings. If you want to extend any of the walks, Try the OS Pathfinder maps, with their 2.5˝ to 1 mile scale. The number of the appropriate Pathfinder map and the grid references are given at the beginning of each walk.

If you are unfamiliar with maps and grid references, here's how to read them. Maps are marked out in numbered squares. The first three figures in the grid reference refer to the numbers at the top and bottom of the map, the last three figures refer to those at the sides. So for example 234567 is read 23.4 along the top or bottom and 56.7 up the side.

Suffolk County Council has a series of attractive walks leaflets, obtainable from Tourist Information Centres, or send an sae for a list and order form to The County Planning Department, St Edmund House, County Hall, Ipswich IP4 1LZ. Tel: 01473-265131.

PUBLIC TRANSPORT

The East Suffolk Line – if it's still running when you read this – has stations at Woodbridge, Melton, Saxmundham, and Darsham, Trimley and Felixstowe, all of which could be used to reach some of the walks. (No trains to Trimley and Felixstowe on winter Sundays). For information about train times, etc, tel: 01473-693396.

Where bus services have been described as 'regular', there is a bus at least five days a week, but frequency of services may range from hourly to once a day. 'Irregular' services mean less than five days a week. Some places only have a bus service on summer Sundays. For information about times of buses, contact Eastern Counties, tel: 01473-253734, or Suffolk County Council Information Line, tel: 01473-265676, Mon-Fri 8.30am-5pm.

Suffolk Public Transport Guide, maps and other useful information, free from County Connexions, County Hall, IP4 1LZ (send sae) or local libraries and Tourist Information Centres.

PUBS

Generally, pubs serve lunch at 12-2pm. Evening meals are more variable. Also, landlords often change so phone numbers are given to enable you to check details. Where a pub's details are different from the norm, information is provided. We have not tried the food in all of the pubs.

EQUIPMENT

Boots are not necessary on any of these walks in good weather, but might be advisable when walking through reed beds. They are certainly recommended on farmland or marshy land after prolonged rain. A walking stick can be handy for waging war on nettles in a few places. Even on hot sunny days, it can be quite chilly on the exposed coast and river walls, so a sweater or windproof jacket would be useful.

BULLS AND OTHER ANIMALS

Bulls are dangerous, but it is illegal for them to be at large in a field crossed by a footpath. If there is a bull in your way, avoid it, report its presence to the Highway Authority, Health and Safety Executive, and the Ramblers Association. In the unlikely event of being attacked by a bull or a dog, you should report it to the police. Cows are usually docile, but be wary if they have young calves, and don't get between a mother and her calf. If a strange dog stiffens, stares and snarls, treat it like royalty – bow out backwards! None of these hazards were met on any of these walks.

FURTHER INFORMATION

If you wish to learn more about the area, there is a bibliography at the end of this book listing all those used in research. Ipswich Museum has a display about the geology of the area with many fossils and rock specimens as well as some wildlife exhibits. I would also commend Dunwich Museum and the many Suffolk Wildlife Trust publications.

THE FORMATION OF THE SANDLINGS

E AST ANGLIA, geologically one of the youngest areas of Britain, is composed of soft chalk rock deposited in the warm shallow seas of the late Cretaceous period, about 130 million years ago. The sea subsided, leaving an area known as London Island, which encompassed what is now East Anglia. Then, about 60 million years ago, the crust of England and Wales began to tilt to the south east, and river sands and marine muds settled over the site of the buried London Island. A deep gulf developed in the 'North Sea' area over which a thick layer of London clay settled. The next few million years saw a gentle folding and tilting of the land when East Anglia was sometimes above sea level and sometimes below. This activity provided the bedrock on which the superficial or drift deposits were laid.

THE VISIBLE LANDSCAPE

London clay does appear on the surface in a few places around the river estuaries but for the most part, the visible landscape of the Sandlings is formed by sands known as crags, laid down over a period of two million years, commencing three and a half million years ago. The shelly, yellowish Coralline Crag is the oldest, deposited in warm, sub-tropical conditions. It appears from around Butley Creek to just north of Aldeburgh, forming a long narrow island in a sea of Red Crag. The Red Crag was deposited mainly on the London clay over two million years ago and covers most of the Sandlings area. It gets its colour from iron oxides and contains an abundance of fossil shells.

Evidence for these materials being laid down under water can be seen in the typical cross-bedded sandy layers in such places as the cliffs at Bawdsey. Fossils in such layers give clues to the type of climate there at the time. The younger Norwich Crag was laid down around one and three-quarter million years ago and occurs north of Orford, particularly in the Sizewell area. It consists of sands interspersed with shell beds, clays and gravels.

As the bed rock of Suffolk is soft and there are no hard rocks to offer resistance, it has eroded fairly evenly; hence the flattish landscape. Around 800,000 years ago, a great river – ancestral to the Thames – flowed north-eastwards across Suffolk. It is thought to have deposited sand and gravel, known as the Kesgrave sands and gravels, and this underlies much of East Suffolk's heathland, mixed with later deposits from the ice sheet which covered Suffolk around 400,000 years ago. The retreat of the ice left behind deposits picked up from the crags, and its meltwaters produced the south-easterly course of the rivers. Erosion provided the alluvial soil of the river valleys. Often peaty, it formed marshlands near the low-lying coast.

CLIMATE

As the climate warmed, at the beginning of the present interglacial phase about 10,000 years ago, the sea level rose once more and swamped the enlarged river estuaries, giving rise to the characteristic broad, shallow estuarine valleys of the Sandlings today. As the warming increased, so the vegetation changed. The tundra-like landscape of birch scrub gave way to woods of pine, birch and hazel and then, around 5,000BC, mixed oakwood, which could also contain elm and lime. It is thought that at this time the temperature was about 2.5°C warmer than it is today. By the time Neolithic man came to settle along the Suffolk coast, the entire county was probably covered in forest. Up until this time, natural changes to the landscape controlled man's settlement of the land, but as he developed technology, it was he that controlled the environment to an increasing extent.

THE FIRST FARMERS

Around 2,500BC, the first Neolithic farmers crossed the North Sea, bringing domestic animals and seed corn, which had originally been cultivated in the Middle East around 7,000BC. The Bronze and Iron Ages saw considerable population growth and many technological developments. This growth and its attendant activity meant increasing forest clearance. Wood was needed for smelting metals, building homes, ships, fences, carts and for making tools and weapons.

By the time the Roman invasion got under way in the first century AD, there had been quite a population explosion and more land was needed to grow food. More and more forest was cut and the land cultivated. This upset the delicate nutrient balance of the light soils, they became infertile, turning to acid podsols. When a patch of land became exhausted, these early agriculturists just moved on and felled another patch of forest. This process was little different from the slash and burn agriculture carried on in some Third World countries today. Aerial photographs show extensive patterns of circles, lines, enclosures, ditches – the remains of these very early cultures frozen forever in the landscape. Centuries of ploughing and levelling have obliterated most evidence of these earthworks at ground level.

Early settlers tended to stay around the Sandlings area because further west, in the woodland of central Suffolk, the heavy clay soil was not easy to work with primitive implements. However, the arrival of the Romans changed all that. They moved right across Suffolk, building farms and homesteads along the river valleys and creating large market settlements at strategic points in the road networks. They vastly extended the area of land under cultivation.

DOMESDAY

Around 400AD, the Roman Empire was in decline and many Romans left, but the population continued to increase as the Anglo Saxon tribes and Scandinavians settled here, creating an urgent need for more land to grow food, which led to a long period of deforestation. After the various Low Country immigrants came the Normans who started to build castles and took an inventory – the Domesday book. This showed Suffolk to be the most populated county in England. It also provided evidence to support a theory about a common Suffolk feature – the large number of isolated churches, thought by some to have been left standing when villages died during the Black Death. A more likely explanation is that they were built by groups of farmers and freemen living on scattered estates within a 'vill', an administrative area. The farmers got together to pay for a church and chose a site that was reasonably accessible to all of them, hence it was unlikely to be near more than one or two estates at the most.

FROM THE MIDDLE AGES

By Norman times, forest clearance had more or less ceased and there were large tracts of heathland that formed an essential part of the medieval economy. The manorial system of land enclosure and commoners' rights was introduced to allow people to graze their animals and keep bees on the heaths and common land. They could cut bracken for animal bedding and thatch, heather for mattresses, walling, medicines and ale-making, and gorse and turf for fuel.

As the Middle Ages advanced, the east coast ports grew and prospered. In the early 14th century, Dunwich was very important, equal in size to Norwich. Ship building, fishing and importing/ exporting spread along the length of the coast. There was increasing enclosure of grassland and heaths. Marshes fringing the rivers and

---

The Normans introduced rabbits in 1135, as a gourmet food supply for the lords of the manor. These early rabbits, from the Mediterranean, were rather tender creatures and had to be cosseted and nurtured, and they did not breed easily. Eventually, some escaped and colonised the heathlands, digging burrows to live in, but their numbers remained low until the mid-19th century when their population took off because of changed agricultural practices and a decrease in such predators as foxes and weasels. They multiplied until the arrival of myxomatosis, when their underground living habits proved to be their undoing. Myxomatosis flourishes underground, and it is interesting to see that many rabbits have now taken to living above ground, in shallow scrapes.

coast were drained and earth banks, planted with coarse grasses to
stabilise them, were built with tidal sluices to control the water levels.

During the 18th and 19th centuries, much heathland, looked on as a wasted resource, was enclosed, to make farms larger, more efficient and easier to work. Many farmers were eager to experiment with new crops, methods and technologies. Some landowners, of course, abused the system and there were battles with commoners over the loss of their rights.

THE 20TH CENTURY

The pace of change accelerated over the last hundred years, leading to the breakdown of traditional patterns of landscape features. In the 1920s and 30s, the Forestry Commission planted vast tracts of heathland with, largely, monocultures of conifers, at Rendlesham, Tunstall and Dunwich. Much of it was devastated by the gales in 1987, just as it was reaching maturity. The 1940's saw areas of heathland disappear under the concrete runways of Bentwaters and Woodbridge air bases. The 1960's and 1970's saw houses and workshops spring up all over Martlesham Heath, and Felixstowe docks spread along the shingle beaches and saltmarshes of the Orwell estuary. And then came the great golf course epidemic.

But by far the largest influence on the landscape has been farming, particularly in the estuaries. Here, the traditional saltmarsh and wet grassland along the river's edge, separated from the dry, sandy valley sides by strips of trees or woodland has been drained, and the trees removed. Flood defences have been improved, and arable land and dry pasture have replaced marshes and heath.

In 1926, a subsidy on sugar beet meant it was grown increasingly instead of other root crops that were used as winter fodder for sheep, so sheep rearing declined. The Agriculture Act of 1947 encouraged farmers to plough up pasture and level the land by filling in ponds and ditches, thus setting the stage for large fields and the use of large machines. Fifty acres was the best size of field for these machines and hedges were costly to maintain, so many farmers removed them. This alone had a significant effect on the landscape, but these changes coincided with the ravages of Dutch Elm Disease, which helped to denude the landscape further.

Thus vast sandy prairies were created which, on dry windy days, produce great dust storms, with soil forming drifts by the roadside. To counteract the consequent loss of soil fertility, enormous quantities of artificial fertilisers had to be employed. These do not improve the soil structure; that requires organic matter, which was naturally provided on the old small mixed farm. The wind-blown light soil dries out so quickly that large irrigation schemes were needed and the old landscape features of hedges, ditches, banks and copses were replaced by gigantic irrigation gantries, acres of plastic sheeting and industrial-style farm buildings.

Britain's entry into Europe, with its Common Agricultural Policy subsidies, resulted in changes in crops grown. Great stretches of the Sandlings burst out in oceans of oilseed rape the colour of lemon curd, and later in swathes of silvery blue flax that, from a distance, look like shimmering lakes.

Then came open air pig production. A welcome improvement for the pigs no doubt, in their detached mini-Nissen hut residences, but the fields are shorn of every blade of greenery.

SUFFOLK IN THE NINETIES.

Now, at last, the pendulum seems to be swinging back. The Wildlife and Countryside Act of 1982 has led to some modification of agricultural policies. The Sandlings area of Suffolk is designated an Area of Outstanding Natural Beauty (AONB) and, in 1988, became an Environmentally Sensitive Area (ESA). This offered farmers financial incentives to turn arable land to grass and manage it less intensively. This has given small livestock farmers an opportunity to expand, and cattle and sheep can again be seen grazing on parts of the coast. It also encouraged tree planting, the reinstatement of landscape features, and

It is possible to estimate the period of enclosure of particular fields by the tree species in the hedges. Ancient hedges might contain a dozen shrub species including, typically, Midland hawthorn, field maple and spindle tree. An Elizabethan hedge would have only four or five species, but a hedge round a 19th-century enclosure would contain only hawthorn and possibly one other shrub, usually elder in the light sandy soils of east Suffolk. Hawthorn is fast growing and not fussy about the soil it's in.

the leaving of uncultivated strips around fields once more.

Left to its own devices land will, depending on climate and availability of seeds, roots and shoots, develop naturally from bare ground to mature woodland. But man usually steps in with landscape management, which is really an accelerated version of natural succession and comes in more varieties. Arable farming, which is deliberately designed to regulate the flora of an agricultural area, is just one variety. Other versions are being strenuously pursued by such bodies as the Sandlings Group, set up in 1983 by the Suffolk Wildlife Trust to ensure the management and appropriate development of commons and heaths in the area. Grazing is a very important feature of managing heaths and grassland and the Wildlife Trust has its own flock of sheep. A large flock of Speckled-faced Beulahs happily chews heather, and even bracken, until with advancing age, their teeth give up. They are then retired to the softer grassland. The flock also contains some dark brown Hebridean sheep who will eat almost anything. The Sandlings Group works closely with The Suffolk Coast and Heaths Project, which came into being in 1993 to establish policies to restore the landscape, develop recreational opportunities and promote public awareness of the value of this vulnerable area.

LANDSCAPE, ECOLOGY AND SPECIAL FEATURES

THE FOUR LARGEST RIVERS of the Sandlings are the Blyth, the Alde/Ore, the Deben and the Orwell. Although each is quite different, they share a number of features – mudflats, saltings and marshes, wet and drained. The smaller rivers Dunwich, Minsmere and Hundred, were all once much larger and more important. Cut off from the sea by shifting shingle and sand, they have now developed into interesting landscape features of marshy reed beds with pools or lagoons just behind the shingle bars, providing important wildlife habitats.

The Orwell is the deepest, widest and straightest estuary, with comparatively steep, fairly well-wooded slopes. It provides a deep, dredged channel from the sea to the busy port of Ipswich, and there is always an interesting variety of shipping to be seen and flocks of sailing craft from the several marinas on both banks.

REED BEDS ON THE DEBEN

Moving northwards, the river valleys become shallower and the rivers wind about in wide, drained, marshy flats between very gently rising slopes. The Deben is particularly tranquil and unspoilt for most of its length, mainly because there are very few places you can reach by car. Both banks are lined with large farm estates whose owners have protected the shores from development. The peacefulness attracts a great variety of birds – wildfowl and waders. The south side of the Deben is bordered by reed beds, saltmarsh and mudflats. The fields behind the ancient flood walls are often lower than the river level. Along the northern shore are a number of sandy beaches and crumbling cliffs which are being eroded and the vegetation deposited onto the beach. Amazing tangles of exposed tree roots along the shoreline show where the water is wearing away the soil, and the trees will eventually topple into the river. There are clumps of reed beds and, below Ramsholt, the land opens out into flat arable plains fringed with remnants of saltings until, reaching the sea, the river narrows and is constrained between shingle banks.

The Alde rises from springs near Brundish and Laxield in 'High Suffolk', and widens out into a broad tidal estuary of mud flats and reed beds, just east of Snape Bridge. Here, a broken line of old flood defences straggles from the Maltings towards Iken Cliff where the south shore rises steeply. Beyond this point are the low hills that were once islands; the church stands on one, and Yarn Hill, thatched with pines, was once a Stone Age settlement. Below Iken, the river widens out further, and as it reaches Aldeburgh, it narrows and turns sharply south, running parallel to the coast, sheltered by the shingle spit of Orfordness, with Sudbourne marshes on the landward side. South of Orford, it becomes the Ore and is joined by the Butley river before reaching the sea at Shingle Street.

The most northerly river of the area, the Blyth, has a very narrow mouth contained by the flood defences protecting Southwold harbour and the village of Walberswick, on the low promontory to the south. Like the Alde, the Blyth bends sharply inland and opens out into a vast expanse of mud flats where the river has broken through the flood defences. It contracts suddenly at Blythburgh where the imposing 'cathedral of the marshes' sits on the promontory commanding the valley.

THE COAST

The Suffolk coast is very open and exposed to tides, currents and winds. Beaches are mostly steep shingle banks, continually shifting, formed into terraces by tides and storms. In a few places, low craggy cliffs crumble onto the beach, forming patches of sand, sometimes for considerable stretches. Fallen trees and other vegetation collect amongst the debris at the base of the eroded cliffs and, as they rot, become colonised by grass and other plants.

Behind the shingle lie marshes, often below sea level, and often protected by sea walls built many centuries ago. From Thorpeness northwards, sand dunes give way to grassy heathland, frequently reclaimed for arable farming. Over the centuries, storms have shifted the shoreline, diverting the course of the Dunwich river and forcing the abandonment of Dunwich Haven, leaving a long, smooth curve of shingle and marsh where once a large sheltered inlet provided the busiest shipping port in the county.

GORSE

Two types of gorse grow in the Sandlings – the tall *Ulex eurpaeus*, commonly called furze, and the short tussocky western gorse, *Ulex gallii*. Gorse is a legume and, like other members of the pea family, has nitrogen-fixing bacteria on its root nodules, so it can enrich the poor, sandy soil around its own root system. Seeds are often spread by ants, which push them along the ground, often along man-made paths. Some get lost and fall into the churned up edges of the paths where they grow into bushes, creating a patchy hedge. Traditionally, gorse had many uses, as a fuel for heating bake ovens and brick and lime kilns. The younger green stalks were crushed and used as cattle fodder.

Further south, both the Minsmere and Hundred rivers silted up and were cut off from the sea. The Hundred had flowed into the northern end of the old medieval port of Aldeburgh, Thorpe Haven. The gradual erosion of Thorpeness contributed to the silting up of the harbour and the blocking of the mouth of the river. The harbour was moved south of the town to Slaughden on the Alde. Although, in time, Slaughden declined as a port, it remained quite a substantial hamlet until it was washed away by the sea at the turn of this century, in spite of the erection of wooden sea defences.

GORSE

Dunwich has disappeared into the sea at the rate of 400 metres in the last 400 years and a series of underwater explorations in the 1970s located various ruins, only to 'lose' them again when tides and currents shifted tons of sand and mud over them. Visibility in this part of the North Sea is very poor because of suspended mud particles transported from the rivers. In spite of this, the diving teams have made many finds on the sea bed, including tree branches complete with leaves, from a wood that was once part of Walberswick.

Orfordness has grown about three miles since the end of the 16th century. Shingle is shifted south along the coast by waves generated by the north easterly winds. Some of the original pebbles were probably supplied by cliff erosion at Dunwich. About 100 years ago a storm lopped a mile off its end, throwing it up onto the beach at Shingle Street. As recently as January 1995, a further chunk broke away and shifted direction during rough weather.

The building of the nuclear power stations at Sizewell has well and truly altered the scenery but Nuclear Electric is trying hard to reinstate the remaining coastline. The water used to cool the turbines in both power stations discharges to the sea, raising the water temperature and providing a local area of sub-tropical conditions for marine life.

Further down the coast at Bawdsey, the remains of another forest lie out to sea, and across the mouth of the Deben an old Roman fort lies off-shore. It is thought that the cliffs of Felixstowe, in Roman times, were about a mile further out to sea. Natural erosion by the elements has been aided by the excavation of septaria for building stone over the centuries. Piles of shingle have been added to this shore in more recent years, and the January storms of 1953 threw up tons of shingle onto the beaches.

BRACKEN

Bracken (*Pteridium aquilinum*) is a bit of a problem because it is fairly indestructable. Few animals like to graze it. Its root system is deep and extensive so even fire doesn't damage it – in fact it can encourage bracken growth by killing off its competitors. If it is cut, it must be cleared for if left, it will decay and provide soil nutrients which will boost further growth, whilst suffocating its rivals. One bracken plant can occupy up to half an acre of land and its underground stems, roots and shoots contain a great store of food. It likes deep, moist soils and relatively frost-free places – frost is one of the few things to which it is vulnerable. In the past, it was cut for animal bedding, which helped to keep it in check, but there are very few uses for it now, though some people compost it.

SHINGLE

Technically, particles between small boulders and sand in size, shingle makes up a considerable part of the Sandlings' coastline. Orford Ness is the best vegetated spit in Europe. Both Orford Ness and Landguard are SSSIs – Sites of Special Scientific Interest – because of their rare and important plant communities. Shingle provides surprisingly varied habitats. Above the high water mark where shingle is more stable, a few plants take root where there are finer grains between the pebbles to provide a root hold. When the plants shed bits, or die, they decompose and humus accumulates, allowing more plants to establish, and gradually quite a variety of species develop until, in places, you may get a thin covering of acid, heathy turf. The early pioneer species have to contend with pretty severe conditions, and therefore, have adopted clever coping mechanisms. There are many specialist species that are very localised and often quite rare; for example sea pea (*Lathyrus japonicus*), sea kale (*Crambe maritima*) and yellow horned poppy (*Glaucium flavum*) . Stinking goosefoot (*Chenopodium vulvaria*) and clustered and suffocated clovers are particularly rare. (*Trifolium glomeratum* and *T. suffocatum*). Other noteworthy plants include sea spurge (*Euphorbia paralias*), sea campion (*Silene maritima*), yellow vetch (*Vicia* lutea) and sea holly (*Eryngium maritimum*). On the grassy shingle heath turf, you may find birds-foot trefoil (*Lotus corniculatus*), bur medick (*Medicago minima*), vipers bugloss (*Echium vulgare*) and hounds tongue (*Cynoglossum officinale*). Flowering plants attract butterflies, including the holly blue, clouded yellow and painted lady. Plant growth is also encouraged by the birds that breed on shingle sites, providing nutrients to the shingle plants.

SIZEWELL
BEACH

LANDSCAPE ECOLOGY AND SPECIAL FEATURES

Heather has a natural life cycle of about 30 years. In its pioneer phase, the first 6-10 years, *Calluna* and other dwarf shrubs together re-colonise bare ground. It grows vigorously during the building phase and in the mature phase, from about 14-25 years, gaps appear in the *Calluna* cover and lichens invade. Anytime after 20 years, the degenerate phase sets in. The old central woody branches die and more lichens move in. Tree seedlings can gain a hold in the bare patches and woodland may start to develop. Or bracken may take a hold and battle it out with the birch scrub for survival.

HEATHS

In the early 1900s, there were 160 square miles of heathland, stretching from Lowestoft to the Orwell; today only 30 square miles remain – mostly concentrated in areas of light, acidic, sandy soils, north of Aldeburgh and east of Woodbridge. Heaths are often a mixture of heathers, lichens, mosses, gorse, broom and grasses, with bracken, birch and pine competing for space. Heather won't tolerate shade, nor will it flourish on nutritious soils where it can't compete with plants hungry for more soil nutrients. The heathers of the Sandlings are mainly ling (*Calluna vulgaris*) and bell heather (*Erica cinerea*) which thrives in hot, dry conditions. *Calluna* will prosper within a wider moisture range and benefits from light grazing.

If heather is heavily grazed, by sheep or rabbits for example, various grasses will take over, creating grassy heathland. Where heather is being re-instated, it needs to be seeded. Dunwich heath is usually the source of seed. The older heather is cut in October and November when the seed is ripe. It is baled and taken to the new site where it is spread in a three-inch layer. This creates a microclimate in which heather seeds can germinate, having fallen out of the bales onto the ground. But, as there is a dearth of heather heathland, and heather takes twenty

CALLUNA
VULGARIS

years to get to the stage you can afford to cut it, there is a need to find a way of getting seed from younger heather without destroying the plant. The Suffolk Wildlife Trust is beginning to try a method used in the north to vegetate old slag heaps. The seed is 'hoovered' off younger heather and spread where it is wanted to grow.

RAGWORT

In the beginning, deciduous forest covered this area, growing on acid brown earth. The soil was kept in balance by the continual circulation of nutrients through the vegetation and soil fauna. Once the trees were felled, this delicate balance collapsed. Rain water draws organic salts from the partly decomposed plant remains in the surface layer of the soil, then seeps down through the mineral layers below, leaving a leached grey 'podsol', deficient in any nutrients – just the sort of soil that heather, but not much else, thrives on.

At various times in the past, farmers have ploughed up this heathland to plant crops, usually trying to improve the soil by adding crag, gravel, lime or marl. But in a very short time, the land proved too poor and was allowed to revert to heathland. However, 20th-century farmers have, by adding tons of artificial fertilizers, been successful in producing high yields of cereals, sugar beet and other crops.

Left to itself, heathland is likely to develop into woodland. Pioneer birch and pine colonise the patches between the heather, and as they grow and shade the heather, it dies off. In time, larger trees such as oak, ash, and elm move in, shading out the birches and, finally, mature deciduous woodland develops.

WOODLAND

There are a great many small woods, some really tiny coverts and shelter belts. Then there are the vast tracts of Forestry Commission conifers – plantations of Scots and Corsican pine and Douglas fir. Some oak and poplars were also planted, but didn't thrive in the loose, sandy soil. These plantations were absolutely devastated by the October gales in 1987, but in the long run the forests have benefited. It has allowed a more enlightened approach to forestry. Fallen trees have been cleared into 'windrows' and left to rot, providing habitats for a great variety of wildlife, including insects, bacteria, other micro-organisms and fungi. All help to decompose the dead trees, providing both soil nutrients and organic matter to improve the soil structure. New trees have been planted between the windrows, but a greater variety of species than before, including some broad-leafed hardwoods. Clearings have been left in places, allowing in more light to encourage flowering plants to get established. These in turn attract butterflies and moths.

All of these woods are extensively managed by Forest Enterprise who encourage people to both use and learn from them. They have provided leaflets of walks and nature trails as well as picnic places.

There are still one or two patches of ancient woodland, notably

---

SCOTS PINE

Most of the plantation pines in Suffolk are Corsican pines (*Pinus nigra maritima*), but there are also plenty of clumps of Scots pine (*Pinus sylvestris*). In cooler times, it grew wild all over Britain, but is now confined to the Highlands of Scotland. In the Sandlings, they have been planted because, although ideally they prefer deep soil, they will also grow in poor, loose, sandy soil. Falling needles eventually create humus which enables other plants to grow. Its tough, curved needles prevent water loss in dry conditions, and pines need less by way of soil nutrients than do broad-leafed trees. Male and female flowers are on the same tree, and the female cones protect the ripening seeds from birds and mammals. The characteristic shape of the older trees is due to the habit of the lower branches of dying off as the tree grows taller.

Resin, a mixture of waxy rosin and turpentine spirit, gives pines their characteristic smell, and is used by the tree to protect any wounds. Man uses it to mix with paint and other chemicals. The timber, which is soft and coarse-grained, has many uses from telegraph poles to chipboard to paper pulp.

Staverton Thicks, with its 400-year-old pollarded oaks cut back about 6-8 feet from the ground, and some venerable hollies, silver birches and rowans among the largest to be found in the whole country.

FIELDS, HEDGES AND VERGES

A great deal of the Sandlings is now covered in fields, containing a variety of crops. You may even be lucky enough to come across the odd meadow full of wild flowers. Those churchyards that are managed as wildlife sites are probably similar in plant content to the old meadows. During the 1960s, when hedges were torn out wholesale, these fields were very often ploughed right up to the very edge, obliterating the uncultivated boundary strips that had provided a haven for many insects and small mammals. In the Sandlings, in spite of massive hedge clearances, there are still remnants of ancient hedgerows that are living evidence of old field patterns and hence, agricultural practices. Really ancient hedges (some may date back to Anglo-Saxon times) often follow parish boundaries or old tracks.

Hedges provide a variety of microclimates and habitats – one side may be in deep shade whilst the other is in full sun. They often sit on earth banks alongside drainage ditches, so provide a home for a great variety of birds, mammals and insects, as well as preventing erosion by wind and rain. They provide wildlife corridors, linking woods and copses, and they certainly provide interest in the landscape.

Roadside verges were once rich grassland, sometimes even semi-woodland, now cut and sprayed to accommodate car drivers and crops. In the past, herds of passing cattle kicked up the soil and grazed the verges, helping to control

SCOTS PINE

their growth. Recently, a more enlightened approach to cutting the banks has meant the return of many flowering plants, snowdrops, primroses, cowslips and mallow, to name a few. Today, salting the roads in winter has led to the appearance of salt-tolerant plants on inland roadsides, their seeds brought from the coast on the wheels of passing vehicles.

RAGWORT

Senecio jacobaea is another plant with few enemies, apart from cinnebar moth caterpillars and Beulah sheep. Because it is a poor competitor, it thrives in areas from which all the more palatable plants have been grazed, particularly where rabbit activity has left bare patches of scuffed earth. Ragwort and cinnebar moth caterpillars act in tandem. The caterpillars can defoliate the plant which then, threatened with extinction, steps up its underground vegetative reproduction; but the resulting plants are puny and don't flower. If there's no flower, there's no seed, so there are less plants and less food for caterpillars next time round. Thus caterpillars starve to death, and ragwort thrives. A wet summer will produce a good crop of ragwort the following year, so cycles of ragwort and cinnebar abundance and scarcity will fluctuate.

SALTMARSH

Salt-tolerant grassland on muddy sediments, deposited by salt water, saltmarsh provides an important transitional vegetated area between tidal mudflats and dry land. Saltmarsh plants have developed some ingenious tricks and devices to enable them to tolerate saline conditions and they act as sediment traps – catching silt and sand from river water. It starts to build up, eventually often forming a kind of low cliff where the soil is stable, allowing a mixed community of plants to grow. There are three zones or levels of marsh. The low marsh lies below the average low tide mark. Only green algae and, sometimes, eel grass (*Zostera marina*) are found here. A bit higher up, as the marsh grades into middle marsh, glasswort (*Salicornia europaea*), cord grass (*Spartina anglica*), and sea aster (*Aster tripolium*) grow. The middle marsh is the part that is mostly submerged every tidal cycle and the soil is waterlogged with salt water. Here grow sea purslane (*Halimione portulacoides*), sea lavender (*Limonium vulgare*), sea arrowgrass (*Triglochin maritima*), sea milkwort (*Glaux maritima*), and sea rush (*Juncus maritima*) and saltmarsh grass (*Puccinellia maritima*). In the high marsh, the soil may dry out completely as it is only submerged briefly when tides are higher than their average. Here you can find members of the Goosefoot family such as sea beet (*Beta vulgaris maritima*) and also sea couch (*Elymus pungens*). Of course, these plants merge and overlap between zones.

It is characteristic of saltmarshes that the surface is split by a network of tidal drainage creeks and salt pans, bare shallow depressions, often containing standing water. Left to develop naturally, saltmarsh would progress to grazing marsh to carr (wet woodland) if not grazed, but in Suffolk this is mostly prevented by the sea walls.

Saltmarsh is very important for birds. It provides grazing for over-wintering flocks of widgeon and brent geese. Linnet and twite forage on the seed heads. It provides roosting sites for waders and nesting sites for redshank, oystercatcher, avocet, black-headed gull, skylark and meadow pipit, amongst others. In some of the more remote parts of our estuaries, the sight and sound of these birds is quite an experience.

SALTMARSH EROSION AT
TRIMLEY THE RIVER ORWELL

LANDSCAPE ECOLOGY AND SPECIAL FEATURES

1

WALBERSWICK

IN THE MIDDLE AGES Walberswick was quite a prosperous port, but ships had to sail up the channel behind the spit from Dunwich Haven. In 1286, Dunwich was sealed off when storm-tossed shingle blocked the mouth of the river. In 1328, the sea breached the spit at Walberswick, allowing the Blyth and its shipping direct access to the sea. A century later, ships were trading from here to Iceland and the Faroes as well as to North Sea ports. The construction of sea walls, for increased grazing and arable land, turned the Blyth estuary into the narrow channel it is today, and towards the end of the last century, the port finally died and Walberswick became just a quiet fishing village.

Sheep and cattle grazed on the heaths and marshes for centuries. The townsfolk had commoners' rights of grazing and freedom to cut the gorse, bracken and heather, which helped keep the heaths in good fettle. In the 17th century, the Lord of the Manor, Sir Robert Brooke, paying scant regard to these rights, ripped out the townspeople's fences to enclose whatever land he wanted for his own animals. The locals took their case to the king – to no avail. In a bitter fight, four men were killed. Some of the peasants were unable to survive economically and either were dispossessed or emigrated.

In the 18th century, there were about 1,500 acres of unenclosed sheepwalks on the Blythburgh and Walberswick estates of Sir John Blois. His tenants were each required to keep at least 800 sheep and fold them regularly at night on land that would benefit from their presence. During the day they grazed the grass and gorse shoots on the heath. In winter they fed upon turnips, and many acres were grown for fodder.

Walberswick Nature Reserve contains one of the largest stretches of fresh water reed beds in the country. Reeds and rushes have been cut from this area for centuries for thatch. You can see how the bracken and birch are encroaching on the heath. Left to its own devices, the area will eventually become woodland, as happened between 1953 and 1972, when myxomatosis decimated the rabbit population and sheep were not being grazed. There was nothing to keep the birch scrub down and within 15 years birch woodland had developed. Birds such as wrynecks, wheatears, woodlarks and whinchats disappeared. However, since the creation of the reserve in 1972, more heath has been opened up, and these birds have returned. Over 100 species of bird have been found to nest in the reserve and there are many winter visitors. There are also many rare insects, including moths and butterflies.

WHERE TO EAT

The Bell, near the village green. The main part of this pub is about 400 years old, with a dining room in the 19th-century extension, and a pretty garden. Children welcome (not in bar). Dogs on leads. Homemade food, reasonable prices. Les Routiers recommended. Tel: 01502-723109.

The Anchor. A residential hotel with bar where good snack meals are served. Bit austere, or tasteful, according to your view. Good interesting bar meals. Children in hall only. No dogs. Small sheltered garden. Tel: 01502-722112.

The Haven, Southwold Harbour. Don't be put off by its rather scruffy exterior (or the mark on the wall at first floor level showing where the water rose to in the 1953 floods!). Descending the steps into the front bar, you enter a gem of a pub, with a small but appealing menu, mainly local fish and a vegetarian dish. The odd-looking empty house next door was built in 1986 by an architect who apparently forgot to put in a sewage system. Perhaps he spent too long in The Harbour at the design stage! Lunches all the year. Dogs welcome, children in front bar. Tel: 01502-722381.

WIND PUMP AT
WALBERSWICK

WALBERSWICK

The Parish Lantern, on the Green. Tearoom, craft shop, sells organic herbs, art gallery upstairs. The 'parish lantern' is the moon, so called in places without street lights, as here. Open: Summer 10am-5.30pm every day. January-March, Fri-Sun 10am-5pm. Tel: 01502-723173.
The Potters Wheel, on the Green. Restaurant-tea room, licensed. Walled garden. Tel: 01502-724468
Mary's of Walberswick. High Street. Pleasant rambling restaurant. Cream teas, high teas and lunches. Prices reasonable. Open Easter-October, Tue-Sun 10am-6pm, Mondays during school summer holidays and Bank Holidays. November-Easter, open Fri-Sun. Tel: 01502-723243.

LOCAL INTEREST
Ferry to Southwold (25p), summer, 9am-12.30pm, 2-5.30 pm.
Shawsgate English Wine Shop, Art Gallery and Heritage Centre, all on the Green. Tel: 01502-722605.
St. Andrew's Church on the way into the village. The church in the 16th century was as imposing as the one at Blythburgh but the decline in shipbuilding and fishing meant lack of funds to keep it up. So the present, smaller one was built, using materials from the larger church which was allowed to collapse into ruins. The tower and some of the old walls are built of rows of cut flint. Inside is a rather nice window panel made from fragments of 14th and 15th century glass, found when the ruins were excavated in 1930.

FURTHER AFIELD
Blythburgh Church. This most imposing building in its position at the head of the estuary earns its name as the cathedral of the marshes. Light pours in through the plain glass windows onto the pale gold pamment floor and whitewashed walls. There is a striking tie beam roof, so well made that it required no repair for 500 years. Some of the original colouring can still be seen and there is a modern replica of one of the angels, above the south porch door.
Wooten's Plant Nursery, Wenhaston, a couple of miles west of the

A12 from Blythburgh. A delightful small family-owned nursery, an extension of their own garden containing some unusual plants at very reasonable prices. Well worth the detour if you are interested in plants.
The Star is a few steps from Wooten's, and is a pleasant unpretentious pub with a nice garden and open views.
Otter Trust, Earsham, Bungay. Open 10.30am-6pm April-October. Feeding times noon and 1pm. £3.50. Wheelchair visitors free. Café and souvenir shop. Tel: 01986-893470.

THE WALK

A generally well-signposted walk through Walberswick Nature Reserve. The route crosses heathland on Walberswick common and runs alongside the Blyth river through Southwold harbour and across ancient sheep walks and marshes.

TRANSPORT

Park: free in the Ferry car park at end of village. Map ref: 499749, Pathfinder 966. Turn east off the A12 about 1½ miles south of Blythburgh onto B1387.
Buses: irregular services from Lowestoft via Blythburgh, and Saxmundham via Yoxford. Summer Sundays from Ipswich.

4½ MILE WALK

Leave the car park by the yellow waymarked footpath at the village end, going inland, and turn right towards Southwold. When you reach the river you will find the ferry hut where you turn left alongside the river. On the left, reed beds and water meadows lead to the gently rising land of the village. Shortly after passing the Harbour pub on the far side of the river, you come to the old railway bridge where you turn left onto the broad track. Away to your right is an old disused wind pump. Follow the tarmac track through reed beds, wet grazing meadows and heathland until you reach Heath House on the outskirts of the village. Just past the house, take the footpath to the right across

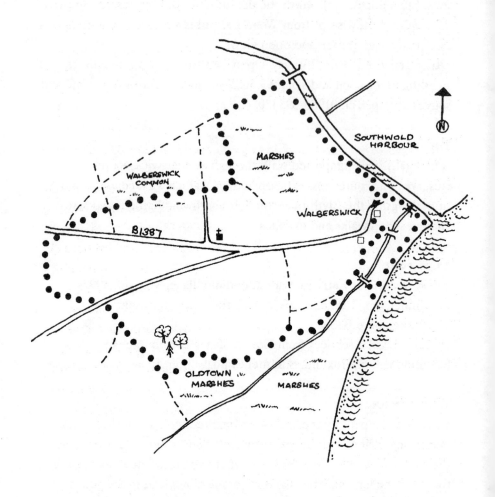

WALBERSWICK

Walberswick Common. When you come to a muddle of paths, including a road leading to the church, keep straight ahead, ignoring all side turnings. After about half a mile, you come to a four-fingered signpost by a dismantled bridge which carried the old railway. Keep straight ahead over land where heather and bracken are competing for space. When you come to the road (busy in summer), turn right and in a short distance you will find the footpath sign on the left, just before the trees. After a few yards, bear right towards a pine belt; the path runs along the edge of the trees. On your left is a grassy heath with scots pines, birches, gorse and bracken trying to gain a hold. The sea can be seen ahead of you. You reach another road and the bridleway continues straight across it on more scrubby heathland with some heather. Follow the English Nature footpath sign until you reach a gate, where you fork left. When you reach the reed beds of Old Town marshes, turn left towards the high ground. The path runs through the reed beds on a board walk, then meanders uphill amongst trees, scrub and brambles – a very pretty route with views down the coast to Dunwich and Sizewell. Just before the path curves round to some white railings, branch right towards the sea and follow this lower path which runs alongside the Dunwich river. You can cross the river and walk along the sea wall, or along the fairly sandy shore, or behind the dunes until you reach the river, then turn inland, passing the fishermen's huts and artists houses, to the car park. Alternatively, continue on the path through the marshes until it eventually curves inland – a bit damp here – towards the caravans. The path goes between these and, at another bridge over the river, bears left alongside the river to arrive at the village nearly opposite the Potters Wheel restaurant. Turn right and follow the road back to the car park.

This walk could be extended by crossing the old railway bridge, and continuing over the marshes and common into Southwold town, then crossing back over the river and either continuing the walk, as above, or cutting it short, returning to the car park.

2

DUNWICH

DUNWICH, like much of the Suffolk coast, is constantly being eroded by the action of waves and tides but it is perhaps more obvious here because of the high cliffs. The fight against erosion has been going on since at least the Middle Ages. It is thought that in medieval times, shingle and brushwood were mixed together and piled at the base of cliffs to mitigate against the action of the waves.

In the 11th century, although half the town had been lost to the sea, a shingle spit had formed south of Southwold, diverting the mouth of the river Blyth to Dunwich and creating a good spacious harbour, the best on the East Anglian coast. In the 12th century, the population was 4,500 – half the size of London – and by the 13th century, Dunwich was a very important port, equal in size to Norwich. Foreign merchants had settled here and the waterfront was busy with shipbuilding, fishing, ships importing and exporting wool, corn, salt, fish, honey, wax, timber and furs. In 1286, a violent storm choked the harbour entrance with shingle; this was the end of Dunwich as a port and its fortunes declined. The Dunwich and Blyth rivers found a new exit to the sea at Walberswick. Since then, the cliffs have crumbled at the rate of one metre a year on average. However, in about 1921, a large sandbank – the Dunwich-Sizewell bank – developed off the coast, reducing the rate of erosion somewhat. Sandy crag with tree roots and other plant debris has collected at the foot of the cliffs in places and has been colonised by grass and other plants.

The Dunwich river has been deflected north of the village, along the back of the shingle beach where extensive marshland has formed. The river runs through Westwood Marshes in the Walberswick Nature Reserve and passes through the eastern edge of Walberswick before disgorging into the mouth of the Blyth. Where the land rises to the north and west of Dunwich, it is covered in forest, mainly Forestry

Commission plantations. Dunwich forest was previously heath except for Scheiller's Grove and Hog's Grove, areas of older woodland within the forest.

The Burnet, or Dunwich, rose is a native of Suffolk, found amongst the sand dunes along this strip of coast. Alexanders abound – they are common on the east coast. They are mediterranean and may have been introduced by the Romans, who ate the stalks like celery.

BURNET ROSE

There are no remains of the Saxon or medieval towns now. The last medieval church collapsed onto the beach at the beginning of this century. The remains of Greyfriars Franciscan Friary, built in 1289, stands on the cliff top. There is an excellent model on display in the museum depicting the medieval town, and its relation to today's coastline.

WHERE TO EAT

The Ship. This has a big pleasant garden at the back with a fig tree and a grassy bank rising to Greyfriars walls. Wide selection of homemade meals, including local fish dishes and vegetarian choices. Reasonable prices. Children and well-behaved dogs on leads welcome. Rooms to let. Tel: 01728-648219.

Flora Tea Rooms. Beach café, renowned for its fish and chips. Basic, clean and airy. Wood panelled walls gaily decorated with tea towels. Large outdoor terrace overlooking car park and bay. Coffee and tea served in large mugs. Childrens menu £2.50. Closed end November-early March. Open during season 10am-5pm. Other times 10am-3pm.

LOCAL INTEREST

Dunwich Museum, St James Street. A splendid little museum well worth a visit – don't miss it. Open daily Good Friday to September.

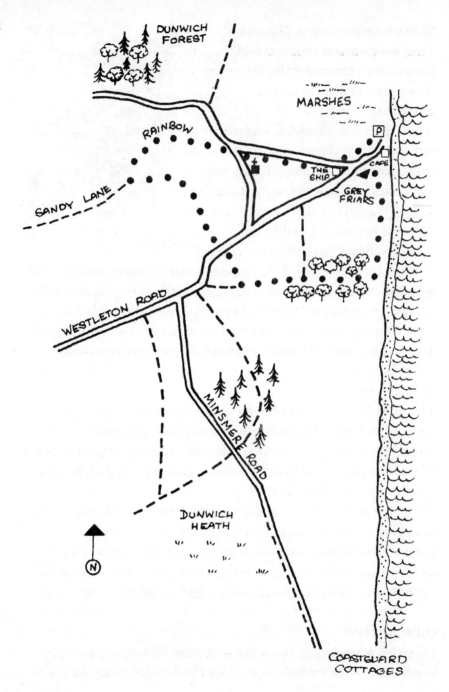

DUNWICH

11.30am-4.40pm October 12-4pm. March weekends only 2-4.30pm.
Free, but donations welcome (in box).
Fresh fish is obtainable from fishermen's hut on beach.

THE WALK

A well worn and waymarked route for most of the way, along cliff tops,
through scrub and woods on the route of an old medieval road into the
town and across attractive well wooded farm land. The route also takes
you along the village street.

TRANSPORT

Park: in the beach car park, on the site of the old Maison Dieu
hospital. Parking is free but donations are requested for local churches
and charities. Map ref: 478706, Pathfinder 966. Leaving the A12 just
north of Yoxford follow the signs through Westleton to Dunwich.
On entering Dunwich, the car park is signposted.
Buses: infrequent Villager service. Tel: 01728-604347. Sunday and
Bank Holiday service from Saxmundham.

2¹/₂ MILE WALK

From the car park, go back to the road. Opposite the garden of The
Ship is a footpath going up to the left. The walls of Greyfriars ruins are
on your right and the cliff to the left through the scrub. Follow the
marked path along the edge of the ruins. This path marks the line of
the medieval town ramparts, and is the last remaining vestige of the
Saxon and medieval towns. The wall is built mostly from beach
cobbles and limestone salvaged from previous buildings. Follow the
path along the cliff until you come to a sunken crosspath known as
Lovers Lane. Turn right and follow the path, ignoring any side
turnings. You pass two sets of iron gates depicting white friars and the
name East Friars. Just after the second pair, by a house on the right
called Whitefriars, take the footpath between tall hedges and follow
this to the road. You emerge just before the road forks into Dunwich.

Turn left, and a few yards along on the right is a gap in the hedge by a telegraph pole. This path leads down the right-hand edge of the field beside a thick hedge, a home for rabbits and many butterflies. Continue through the second field, which is very sandy with heathlike grassland breaking through round the edges. At the far side of the field, go through the hedge just past a house called Walnut Tree Cottage. This brings you to a lane called the Rainbow. Turn right along the broad level track to the road where you get a good view across the marshes to the shingle banks of the beach. Turn right and walk back through the village to the car park.

There are many other walks that can be added to this short one. For example, from half way along Sandy Lane you can continue via Mount Pleasant Farm to Dunwich Heath and return through Greyfriars Wood or along the beach. For trails through Dunwich Forest, leaflets are obtainable from National Trust premises on Dunwich Heath or Westleton Post Office or Forest Enterprise in Tangham Forest. There are footpaths all the way to Walberswick with an alternative return route if you are looking for a really long walk. The Parish Lantern in Walberswick has attractive sketch maps of walks in the area. For the dedicated walker/ naturalist with a whole day to spare, much varied and interesting country waits to be explored.

ALEXANDERS

DUNWICH

MINSMERE, EASTBRIDGE AND WESTLETON

3

THE START OF THE WALK from Eastbridge takes you along the wet grazing meadows initially created by the Minsmere Levels Drainage Trust in 1813, when they dug the Minsmere New Cut to drain the marshes and channel the river to the newly-built sluice at the beach. There is a good view of the New Cut from the road bridge just north of the Eel's Foot. In 1940, the land was deliberately re-flooded as a defence against the threat of a German invasion.

In 1947, the RSPB rented 1,500 acres of this land from the Ogilvie family to create a reserve, and discovered that avocets, encouraged by the lack of human activity during the war years, had started to breed there – the first time they had bred in Britain for over 100 years. Later, marsh harriers – rare in this country – began to breed in the reed beds.

There is an entrance to the reserve (permit holders only) at the sluice, and a public hide along the beach. The scrape was constructed in 1962 on the remains of the old broad, created at the beginning of the 18th century, when the mouth of the Minsmere river silted up. Gravel underlying the heather and birch of the Minsmere heathlands was used to construct the scrape. The reserve contains 400 acres of reed bed populated by marsh harriers, bitterns, bearded tits, sedge, reed and grasshopper warblers and, occasionally, Savi's warbler – a rare visitor.

The RSPB has been buying large areas of farmland and restoring it to heather and acid grassland. This will eventually provide 900 acres of heath, suitable breeding ground for nightjars, stone curlews and woodlarks. On the beach and dunes, you will find fenced off areas to protect the young of ringed plovers and little terns from walker's boots and dogs. Stonechats, linnets and whitethroats nest in the bushes on the dunes and visiting migrants include wheatears, whinchats, meadow pipits, goldcrests and a variety of warblers.

The 1987 hurricane devastated the woodland areas of the reserve but clearings created by the winds have allowed more light to reach the ground, so plants and shrubs have grown, encouraging blackcaps, nightingales and garden warblers to move in. Some of the woodland is being left to regenerate naturally, providing shelter for red deer and muntjac, but some of the conifer stands are being cut back to help heath regenerate and allow flowers to colonise. Amongst the interesting flora are southern marsh and common spotted orchids and the rare marsh sowthistles, which are yellow and don't look much like thistles! Otters were introduced in 1988 and are thriving. Frogs and toads are numerous, and lizards and adders can be found on the heath where damselflies, dragonflies and butterflies abound.

The RSPB records around 220 species seen in the reserve each year, about 100 of which breed in the scrape. There are also more than 600 plant species recorded, making this an extremely rich wildlife area.

Dunwich Heath, an important relic of extensive heaths in this area, was once grazed by flocks of sheep by day which were folded on arable land at night – a mobile manuring system! Many of the names used around here are reminders of the long association with sheep rearing – Westleton (sheep) walks and Sheep Wash Lane, for example.

Once sheep rearing declined, rabbits continued to graze the land to some extent. Rabbit warrens were established in Minsmere, Westleton, Middleton and Dunwich by a grant of free warren in 1265, and were used for food. However, the open expanse of heathland you see today is the result of enthusiastic management efforts by the National Trust warden rather than of grazing animals. Management has meant shifting many tons of shingly soil and constantly 'swiping,' or uprooting by hand, bracken and birch seedlings – the latter done with the help of local volunteers. The result is the impressive spread of heathers and the low Western gorse, which stretches in purple and gold waves to the sea, giving shelter to linnets, larks, meadow pipits and yellow hammers, and even, I believe, the odd glow-worm. About 90% of the heather here is ling but cross leafed heather, *Erica tetralix*, normally preferring wet soil conditions, flourishes along the dry cliff top.

Dunwich Heath merges with the heathlands of Westleton and of the Minsmere reserve where silver birches have been allowed to grow amongst the heather, creating a very attractive landscape.

WHERE TO EAT

Eel's Foot. Said to be a derivation of 'Neales boot' (those are them displayed along the pub wall). John Neale was a priest who kicked the devil out by putting him, in the form of an eel, in his boot and kicking it out to sea. This happened one year when a lot of eels – thought to be the devil in disguise – had the villagers worried. An unpretentious, friendly little pub with good value, home cooked bar snacks. Dogs allowed in the bar. Tel: 01728-830154.

National Trust Tearoom, part of the complex in the Coastguard Cottages Dunwich Heath. Light lunches and snacks,good homemade cakes. Open November-March, Sat and Sun 11am-4pm; April-June, September, October; Wed-Sun 11am-5pm; July and August, daily 11am-5pm. July and September, takeaway service Mon and Tue.

TOWARDS SIZEWELL FROM DUNWICH CLIFFS

MINSMERE, EASTBRIDGE AND WESTLETON

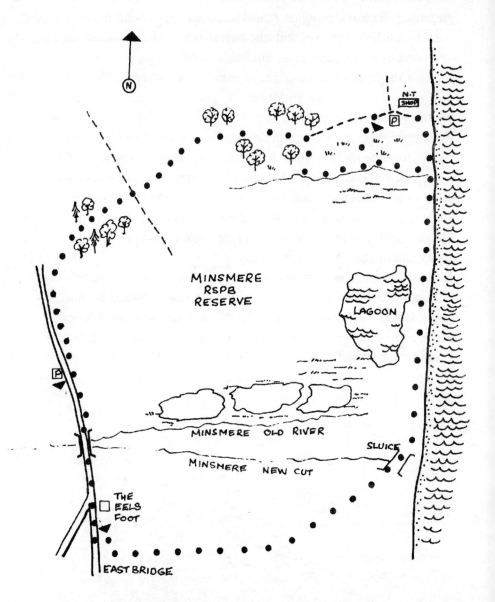

N

MINSMERE
RSPB
RESERVE

LAGOON

MINSMERE   OLD   RIVER

MINSMERE   NEW CUT

SLUICE

N.T
SHOP

P

P

THE
EELS
FOOT

EASTBRIDGE

MINSMERE, EASTBRIDGE AND WESTLETON

LOCAL INTEREST

National Trust. Information room and lookout are above the tearoom, there is a stairlift. The shop sells a good selection of National Trust goods. Toilets for disabled people next to shop.

Disabled people who have difficulty walking can borrow a battery-operated vehicle to go around the heath and its environs. This service is free but if you have enjoyed yourself, a donation would be appreciated. To book the vehicle, contact the Warden, tel: 01728-648505.

RSPB Reserve. Open every day except Tuesdays, 9am-9pm or dusk. Day permits available on arrival. Charge for non-members. Wheelchair users can also get to some of the hides. The Reserve also runs a number of guided walks and educational events from April to September for which a small charge is made. Booking essential. Tel: 01728-648218 for further information.

Leiston Abbey was built on its present site in 1363 when the building materials were brought from the former 'unhealthy swampy site' at Minsmere. The beautiful 15th-century tithe barn has been converted into a concert hall which belongs to Pro Corda, a school of chamber music. It runs residential courses for young musicians who are accommodated in Leiston Abbey House. The ruins of the abbey are most impressive and are in the care of English Heritage.

THE WALK

A mostly easy walk through wet meadows, marsh, woods, heathland and some arable land. The route of the walk is mainly along the outside of the RSPB Reserve.

TRANSPORT

Park: beside the road just north of the bridge over the river, north of the pub in Eastbridge. Permission can be obtained from the landlord at the Eel's Foot to park in the car park, or you can park on Dunwich Heath (£1.50, National Trust members free). Map ref: 453665 Pathfinder 987. For Eastbridge, turn off the B1122 from Leiston just past Leiston Abbey. For Dunwich Heath, take the Dunwich road from Westleton and just before you reach Dunwich turn right onto the Minsmere Road. Map ref: 477677, Pathfinder 987.

Buses: infrequent Villager service to Eastbridge. Tel: 01728-604347.

5 MILE WALK

Cross the bridge and, passing The Eel's Foot, turn left up the lane and take the footpath on the left with a sign to Minsmere sluice 1½ miles. The raised path runs between reclaimed marshes and arable land. You cross a stile and veer right onto the broad track running alongside a drain. You pass through three gates and at the fourth, go left. From here, to your right, you can see what are thought to be the ruins of the first Leiston Abbey. Just before the sea wall is the red brickwork of the sluice. Cross it and turn left onto the path towards Dunwich Heath with its row of white coastguard cottages. The very sandy path runs between the dunes and the banks of the nature reserve. You can always walk on the beach, which has easier stretches of firm sand. There is a public hide along this path, with spectacular views of the lagoons in the reserve and their bird life – well worth bringing binoculars. On reaching the rise up to Dunwich Heath, you can climb up to the National Trust shop, tea room and toilets or continue along the path to your left along Docwra's Ditch. If you go up onto the heath, you rejoin the track by taking the path behind the toilets which winds downhill to the left and joins the other path along Docwra's Ditch (named after a previous Trust warden not, as I'd fondly imagined, some early English heroine!). Turn right here and follow a very pretty route with the ditch and reed beds on your left and the steep rise of the heath on the right. At the end of the water, you come to a small clearing. Follow the path that turns sharply round to the left, where the water reappears and the path meanders through birch woods. Beware of tripping over tree roots when admiring the extremely pretty scenery! The path ends at a T-junction with a bench and NT sign; turn left through some posts and across open heather to

THE EELS FOOT
EASTBRIDGE

more birch woods. When you come to another T-junction, turn left and continue to a crossroads with the metalled road. Cross over the road and continue on the bridleway over fields. You will soon see the whole of the Sizewell power station complex ahead to your left. The white dome of Sizewell B on its blue plinth is a not unpleasing building and has the advantage, from some angles, of obscuring the hideous concrete bunker of Sizewell A. That said, it hardly enhances a most beautiful landscape. The track goes downhill quite steeply and enters a wood. Through the wood you come to a road with another entrance to the reserve on your left. Continue ahead along the road which is lined with coppiced limes. Follow this to your car or continue into Eastbridge and the pub which you reach shortly after crossing a bridge over the Minsmere river and the New Cut.

If you wish to lengthen this walk turn right onto the footpath directly after crossing the bridge over the river and follow the directions for the Westleton to Eastbridge walk from this point.

4 MIDDLETON, WESTLETON AND EASTBRIDGE

BETWEEN THESE THREE VILLAGES and to the north and east of Westleton, is one of the largest remaining expanses of heathland in the Sandlings. The underlying geology is smooth quartz and flint pebbles, laid down in beds entirely of pebbles at their deepest but increasingly mixed with white sand towards the surface where they are overlain with glacial sands and gravels. There is a theory that these Westleton Beds are relics of ancient beaches and they stretch for about ten miles around Westleton, creating an undulating area of dips and rises covered in *Calluna* heather.

Fergus Menteith Ogilvie, a distinguished Suffolk ornithologist, knew these heathlands at the turn of the century, before commercial forestry had really started and sheep were still grazing the Walks. He described a great deal of the coastal land between Sizewell and Walberswick as being rough moorland mixed with some arable and marsh land with very few trees; indeed the higher ground which was almost entirely covered in heather, seemed more like areas of the Yorkshire moors. Some parts were dominated by bracken and gorse, as they are today. Where the moorland edges were ploughed up, the soil was so poor and stony it was often allowed to revert back to heathland. In earlier times, local crag was used to improve the light soil for growing crops. The Ogilvie estate papers record that crag and gravel was dug from pits and used when establishing farms and planting trees on the estate in the middle of the 19th century.

The 47 hectare Westleton Nature Reserve is one of the few remaining extensive areas of *Calluna* heathland. Management of the reserve includes controlled regular heather burning, designed to assess the best burning cycle to maintain the greatest diversity of age

THE VILLAGE POND
AT WESTLETON.

structures needed to provide suitable habitats for all the creatures who normally live in the heathland. Bracken and scrub clearing and grazing are regularly undertaken, and as a result, this is one of the best managed heaths in Britain.

From the coast, the Minsmere river runs inland through a broad, marshy valley of wet grazing meadows, and narrows as it approaches Middleton. On the higher ground of the valley sides the land has been ploughed for arable farmland. Middleton, on the edge of the marsh is nowhere more than 10m above sea level. Westleton, which gets its name from a Norse settler, Vestildli (Vestildli's Tun), lies a good bit higher, some of it being 25m above sea level. The Minsmere valley contains a rich flora and a great variety of birds. Various marsh orchids can be found around Eastbridge, including the very rare albino variety of the Southern Marsh orchid. The scarce Great Butterfly orchid has been found around Westleton – very striking greenish white flowers with a strong sweet smell.

Darsham Marshes reserve, between Westleton and Darsham is another important refuge for marshland flora and fauna. Given to the Suffolk Wildlife Trust in 1982, it was old grazing meadows drained by dykes. Now overgrown by plants, it includes a rare aquatic liverwort.

The Bell, Middleton. Low beamed bar with large grassy garden overlooking open country. Usual pub fare; local caught fish and chips, Cromer crab salad, lasagne etc. Children and dogs welcome. Cheaper childrens portions available. Tel: 01728-648286.

The White Horse, Westleton. Rather austere Victorian red brick exterior belies a warm, comfortable pub with log fire under copper canopy. Classical music. Reasonably priced varied menu including local fish dishes and a vegetarian choice. Pretty walled garden at back. Offers B&B. Tel: 01728-648222.

The Crown, Westleton. Attractive, with good food reputation. Three restaurants, conservatory, patio and garden. Children welcome in restaurants. Dogs allowed in bar. Tel: 01728-648777.

The Eel's Foot, Eastbridge (see page 39).

Westleton Crafts & Tea Room. Tea and coffee served all day.

Central House Restaurant and Tea room – open for teas Sat and Sun throughout the year, also for Sun lunch. Summer opening times more flexible. Tel: 01728-648297.

LOCAL INTEREST

Middleton is a very pretty village round a green with a white thatched pub and an attractive mosaic village sign with a cockerel on one side, the church on the other.

Westleton, another pretty village, is more developed than Middleton. There is a large triangular green at the north end of the village sloping down to the duck pond. By the gate of the large churchyard are two lime trees, one of which is a small-leaved lime, a native of ancient woodlands and hedgerows but now fairly rare.

There is a second hand bookshop in the Primitive Methodist chapel, just opposite the Crown. It is stuffed with books, not just on shelves. If you get

MARSH ORCHID

exhausted from squeezing between them you can collapse into the dilapidated old arm chair and have a good read. The proprietor may even offer you a mug of coffee.

Darsham Marshes Reserve Otters, frogs, toads and many birds of prey including little, barn, long and short eared owls. There are southern marsh orchids, marsh marigolds, valerian and ragged robin. There is a footpath through the reserve which is open all the time and can be very muddy. On the left hand side of the Westleton to Darsham road.

Long Shop Museum, Main Street, Leiston. Fascinating museum commemorating the 200 years of industrial history of the Garrett Works and the town of Leiston, which was a small village in 1778 when Richard Garrett started work as a bladesmith. Housed in a Grade II listed building, it is one of the earliest production line buildings in existence. It was built in 1852 to house the manufacture and assembly of engines. Over the years, Garrett's manufactured a tremendous range of products from agricultural implements to traction engines, and anti-aircraft guns to trolley buses. Gift shop and picnic garden. Open daily April-October 10am-5pm. Tel: 01728-832189/830550.

Leiston Abbey (see page 41).

RSPB Reserve (see page 41).

MIDDLETON TO WESTLETON WALK

An easy, mostly level walk on sandy paths. Well signposted.

TRANSPORT

Park: Middleton village by the Bell pub. Map ref: 429677, Pathfinder 987. From the A12 at Yoxford take the B1122 towards Leiston and turn left onto B1125 for Westleton. To reach Middleton village take a left turn off this road. The walk could also be started from Westleton – park in the village, map ref: 440692.

Buses: from Saxmundham to both villages on Wed, Sat and Sun.

Trains: on the East Suffolk line stop at Saxmundham and Darsham. Tel: 01473-693396.

MIDDLETON, WESTLETON AND EASTBRIDGE

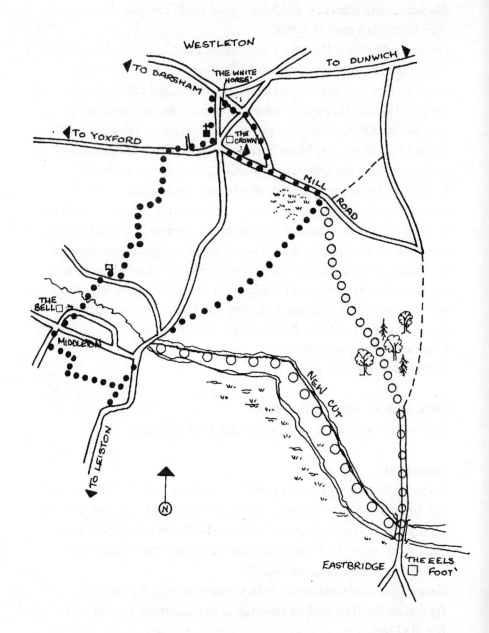

MIDDLETON, WESTLETON AND EASTBRIDGE

With your back to the pub, walk straight ahead. You pass the primary
school on the right and go through a gate on the left of the road,
following the footpath with a cypress hedge along the left-hand side.
Cross the wooden footbridge over the Minsmere river and an easy
stile. (In May, the path was rather overgrown with cow parsley and
overhung with willow, poplars and hawthorn, making it rather daunting
if you are five foot nothing). Eventually you come to a road opposite
some farm buildings; turn right and pick up the footpath again on the
left past the end of the buildings. The broad track crosses the fields in
a series of dog-leg bends. You will see the large, thatched, 14th-century
church away to your right in Westleton village. When you reach the
road, turn right and at the end of a high conifer hedge, you will find a
stile to the left. Climb it and cross the meadow towards the church,
through the gate and across the churchyard to the road, opposite The
Crown. Turn left, passing the Jubilee Clock on your right, and at the
end of this road you come to The White Horse. Turn right here,
passing between the village green and the duck pond. Turn right into
the main street. At the far end of the street, past The Crown again,
turn left up Mill Road which takes you across Westleton Common.

After about ½ a mile, you come to a junction of paths. If you wish a
longer walk, take the footpath that goes at a slight angle uphill to the
right of the road (see directions for Westleton/Eastbridge walk on
p.00); otherwise turn directly right onto a wide stony bridleway going
downhill between banks of gorse. The heathland gives way to fields
and when you reach a road, turn left. You follow the road across
Reckford Bridge and round a sharp bend to the left. Opposite a garage,
you will find a footpath sign into a field on your right. Follow up the
side of the field to the bridleway at the top and turn right onto it.

(If you prefer not to walk about ¼ mile on a rather busy road, turn
right just before the bridge up a quiet road and just past the farm you
passed on the way to Westleton, turn left onto the footpath retracing
your steps over the river and back to Middleton village.)

MIDDLETON, WESTLETON AND EASTBRIDGE

Follow the bridleway along the right side of the field, go through the hedge at the end, turn right along the edge of the next field and at the end, turn left and follow the track down to the road. Turn right and right again into the village street which will bring you back to the pub.

WESTLETON TO EASTBRIDGE WALK

A most attractive walk, through some of the best remaining heathland in Suffolk, and the woodlands of the Minsmere reserve and attractive wet meadowland. This walk can be done on its own or as an extension to the Middleton Westleton walk, or possibly as an extension to the Minsmere walk.

TRANSPORT

Park: If starting from Westleton, park in the village. If starting from Eastbridge, park at the roadside just north of the bridge over the Minsmere river. Map ref: 453665, Pathfinder 987.

4½ MILE WALK

From Westleton village, take the road up by the side of the post office. After it joins Mill Lane, you come to a junction of tracks, with Hardpiece Lane on the left. Fork right onto a footpath which runs uphill, between high gorse bushes. Cross a stile and in a while, the path becomes stony and descends quite steeply down hill, passing through birch and pine woods for about half a mile. When you come to a track coming from the left, turn right onto it and continue past the entrance to the RSPB reserve. Continue more or less straight ahead on the surfaced lane until you come to a bridge with metal rails, turn right immediately after it into the meadow. The path actually goes along the top of the New Cut river bank which, in summer, may be too overgrown. If so walk, along the right-hand edge of the wet meadows with a ditch lined with various water plants on your right. Water lilies, iris, water mint, teasels, tansy and water plantain were all seen in August. You cross over, round or through several gates until you come

to a barbed wire fence that you cannot cross. You must cross the
narrow ditch to your right and climb onto the river bank. The path
here, for about 100 yards is, in summer, somewhat overgrown with
giant rhubarb, nettles and thistles, but it's not impossible as the path
beneath the vegetation is quite broad, so persevere. The rhubarb
disappears, the nettles get shorter and then die out and you are on
shortish grass till you get to a stile, then on a flat grassy bank all the
way to the road.

At the road, turn right, cross the bridge and after about 150 yards
you will find the bridleway singposted to the right. Follow this broad
track which passes through arable fields then rises up onto the
heathland and is bordered by gorse all the way back to the lane, where
you turn left and walk into Westleton village.

WESTLETON
HEATH

5 SAXMUNDHAM, KELSALE AND CARLTON

SAXMUNDHAM, on the old A12, is on the boundary between what John Kirby, in *The Suffolk Traveller* in 1735, described as the Woodland and the Sandlands. In the time of Henry VIII, extensive oak woodlands in the area provided timber for the new quay at Slaughden, and its growing shipbuilding industry. By the 18th century, the land had become heathland and was being extensively improved by the practice of marling – spreading marl or shelly crag, to make the soil suitable for agricultural use. Arthur Young, the agricultural writer, was bemoaning the fact that much of the land between Woodbridge, Orford and Saxmundham was 'wasted', meaning that it was still largely warren, sheep walk, common or heath. He was an enthusiast for enclosing and improving the land for cultivation. Others protested that the land was so poor that it was best to leave it alone. Where it had been split up and improved, it was later allowed to return to heathland. Apparently, lambs grazing on it tended to get rickets. However, there

KELSALE CHURCH
LYCH GATE

was a chemist, one Edward Packard, working in Saxmundham, producing fertilizers from bones. He was quick to see the potential of Professor Henslow's discovery of coprolites, then thought to be fossilized animal dung and other remains, and he bought an old mill in Ipswich to produce it commercially.

During the agricultural depression of the 1800's, there was high rural unemployment in this area. The unrest this caused was exacerbated by the introduction of agricultural machinery. On Boxing Day in 1838, five to six thousand people gathered near Bigsby's Corner to hear the Chartist speakers and then march to Leiston. Nowadays, the land around Saxmundham is well cultivated but the banks and waysides of the area are thick with primroses in the spring.

Kelsale was recorded in Domesday and consisted of two manors, one on either side of the shallow valley created by the Fromus, a tributary of the Alde, which runs parallel with the old A12. The largest manor, by the church, was well wooded and supported 60 pigs.

It is not known for certain what the farming landscape would have looked like at the time, but Norman Scarfe (in *The Suffolk Landscape*) suggests there may have been scattered farms linked to the common grazing at East Green on the higher ground. Alternatively, there may have been a settlement around where the guildhall is now, and probably where the Norman market was located.

The Victorian restoration of Kelsale church included the hilltop on which it stands. From what was described in the Parish Church Guide as a 'stark, pine scattered' hill it became a 'mellow rise' with a variety of mature trees amongst the old houses. At some time, a vineyard was planted adjacent to the church. Kelsale is situated on a pocket of clay and there are several disused clay pits around the village. The clay was dug to mix with the lighter soils for agricultural purposes.

WHERE TO EAT

The Poacher's Pocket, Carlton. Attractive small village pub with picnic tables and a small enclosed garden. Variety of homemade dishes, including a vegetarian option. Specialise in French and Belgian super strength beer. Closed Mon except Bank Holidays. Well behaved children and dogs on leads welcome. Tel: 01728-602174.

White Hart, High Street, Saxmundham. Very much a local. Very large front bar room with tables around the edge of a dance floor. Small cosy bar at the back. Friendly Yorkshire landlord. Les Routiers recommended. Dogs welcome on a lead. Open all day. Tel: 01728-602009.

Queens Head, High Street. Another local, pleasantly old fashioned large long bar with a no smoking area. Large varied menu with some interesting vegetarian options. Regret no dogs. Tel: 01728-602856.

Old Bell, High Street, Saxmundham. Slightly down-at-heel but delightful Georgian hotel with comfortable armchairs and imaginative menu. Generous helpings. Childrens menu, Italian wines. A few tables on the small patio. Dogs welcome. Tel: 01728-602331.

Hayloft Tea Rooms, High Street, Saxmundham. Delightful front room (non smoking) with brick fireplace separating it from the back room which was the stables. Open shop hours all the year. Closed Thursday afternoons and Sundays. Tel: 01728-602895.

LOCAL INTEREST

Kelsale Church A very ancient church with Victorian restorations making it an 'Arts and Crafts movement period piece'. The Arts and Crafts movement of the late 19th century centred on William Morris, and advocated the renewed use of handicraft and simple decoration. The stained glass windows are unusual and most attractive. The panels in the north window were designed by William Morris and Burne Jones. The unusual lych gate dates from 1891 and stands at the end of one of several avenues of limes which were originally pleached (trained and plaited onto wires).

FURTHER AFIELD

Lady's Mantle Meadow, SWT reserve four miles west of Saxmundham.

Pound Farm, Woodland Trust are creating new woodlands on arable land. Three miles north west of Saxmundham, very near Lady's Mantle Meadow. Open to the public.

THE WALK

A pleasant easy walk through mostly farmland with some very short stretches on quiet roads. The pretty village of Kelsale and its church is on the route and worth a visit.

TRANSPORT

Park: any side street near where the railway bridge crosses the main road. Map ref: 387633, Pathfinder 986. Turn off A12 Saxmundham bypass onto B1121, into the town centre.
Buses: regular service from Ipswich and Lowestoft.
Train: to Saxmundham station.

5 MILE WALK

Through the white gate by the railway bridge you will find the footpath. It crosses a stile into a field where you keep to the right, following the railway embankment. Leaving the field, the path narrows between very tall hedges. You come to a stile that crosses the railway, then over another stile. The path, not very distinct now, follows round two sides of a field and emerges onto a road. Turn right here and after quite a short distance, you will find a footpath to the left; the sign is hidden in a ditch. (If you come to the drive of Hill Farm; turn back and you will find the footpath running along the

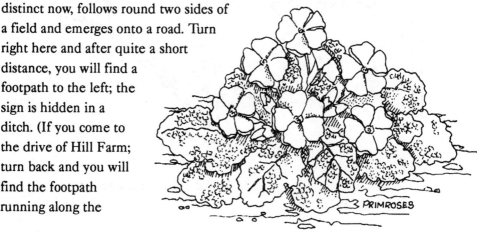

PRIMROSES

SAXMUNDHAM, KELSALE AND CARLTON

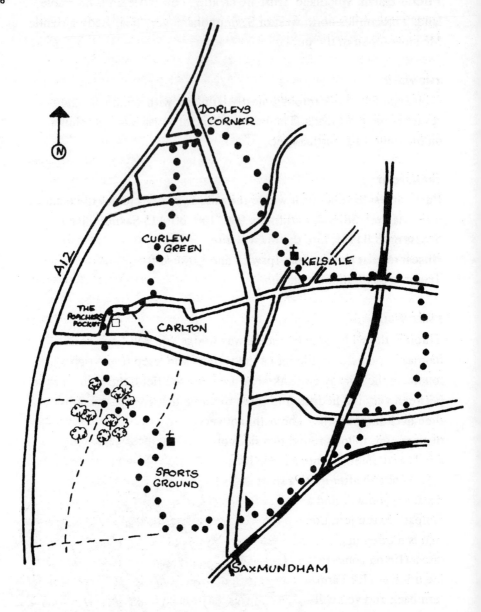

SAXMUNDHAM, KELSALE AND CARLTON

hedge.) At the end of the field, turn left then go through a gap in the hedge and turn right, skirting a pond. The path continues along fields until, reaching the road, you turn left towards Kelsale. When you get into the village, turn right up Dennys Lane to the church. The churchyard is a wildlife sanctuary specially noted for its spring flowers. The path continues to the left of the church, then to the right up some steps, alongside the churchyard and out onto a road where you turn right. A short distance along on the left, you'll find a footbridge over the ditch. Cross this and follow the broad path winding through fields to come out on the main road into Saxmundham at Dorley's Corner. Cross over and take the lane down beside the house. About 100 yards along, a signpost in the hedge on your left directs you through a gate and up the side of a field and continues over fields to a couple of derelict cottages. This is Curlew Green Farm. Cross over the road and follow the footpath through trees and across a stream. When you come to a field, turn right, follow round the field to Rosemary Lane. Turn right and follow the road round to The Poacher's Pocket. Carry on past this pub to a road going across, on the far side of which is a footpath sign pointing straight ahead down Sandy Lane. After a while, this broad, hedged track crosses over a stream and here you turn immediately to the left. When you emerge from the trees, you will see the stripey Tudor brick tower of Carlton church ahead. Head towards it around the edge of the field. The signposted footpath goes to the right, round the outside of the churchyard, to a stile. Over this, the path skirts the field, but you can cut across it and then across the sports ground. At the far side of the field, cross another stile and continue along the edge of a new housing development, cross a new road and turn right at some railings. Cross the bridge over a ditch, and the path runs between a fence and hedge, coming out to the road on a new estate. Turn left and, near the end of this close, the footpath goes between two bungalows and turns right. Follow it onto an older road (Fairfield Road), turn left and you come down onto the main road near the railway bridge where you started the walk.

SAXMUNDHAM, KELSALE AND CARLTON

6

THORPENESS TO SIZEWELL

JUST SOUTH OF THORPENESS was the medieval port of
Thorpe Hythe at the mouth of the River Hundred – now just a
ditch draining into the sea. It silted up in the mid-16th century and a
new quay was built at Slaughden, south of Aldeburgh. In the early
1800s, the Hundred River was drained to provide grazing, and up until
the beginning of this century, it formed a large, shallow tidal delta.
In 1910, it flooded, which gave Glencairn Stuart Ogilvie the idea of
creating a model holiday village at Thorpe, then a small fishing hamlet.
He dammed the river mouth and created the Meare as a boating lake
for his mock Tudor village, with it's distinctive water tower, the House
in the Clouds, and windmill. The mill pumped water to the House in
the Clouds, until Thorpeness was connected to the mains water supply
in 1963. The mill is now a Heritage Coast information centre.

The walk doesn't take you quite as far as Sizewell village but there
is some interesting history to the area. The name Sizewell comes from
the Anglo Saxon *Sisa's well*, suggesting an early settlement there. In the
16th century, it was a fishing port and in the 18th century, the beach
with sandy cliffs and dunes merged with the heath and marsh behind,
stretching back to Leiston Common. A desolate place, it was notorious
for smuggling. Today this stretch, extending northwards past Minsmere
to Walberswick and beyond, tailing off to the south at Thorpeness, is
the only area of Suffolk still to have dunes with Marram grass.

At one time, the local squire planted pine trees on Leiston and
Sizewell commons, which provided work for the unemployed as well as
shelter for his game birds. Between 1946 and 1949, 146 acres of these
heaths were ploughed up by a local farmer who then had to add 15 tons
of chalk per acre to produce reasonable crops. He was not the first to try
to improve the thin heathland. The Ogilvie family who lived in Sizewell
Hall spread shelly crag into the land they cultivated. There are

numerous disused pits in the area and Shellpit cottages, which you pass going through the walks, must have got their name from the crag pits.

In 1961 work was started on construction of the first nuclear power station on the old Sizewell warren. This is an area of Norwich Crag which is composed of patches of almost pure sand interspersed with very shelly fossiliferous beds, as well as clay and gravel. When excavations were underway to build Sizewell B, a shelly patch was found to contain remains of elephant, horses, matadon, deer and voles, as well as a variety of fish, estimated to be nearly two million years old.

The dunes in front of the power stations, known as the benthills – from the dune grasses that grow on them – and all through Sizewell down to Thorpeness, have a rich distinctive flora of tiny flowering species. Where they have been disturbed by the building works, they are being reinstated by the University of East Anglia in collaboration with Nuclear Electric. Fifty species, such as various stonecrops, blue sheepsbit and harebells, birds-foot trefoil and rest-harrow, have been planted from seeds taken from the area before the work started.

The environment around the power stations is continually monitored for any increased radiation. All that has been registered so far has been related to the Chernobyl accident and from Chinese weapons testing. There are regular checks on samples of soil, grass, sea water and sea bed sediment, local fish, honey and milk. Outlying farms are used as control centres. The testing is done from the laboratory at Leiston and duplicated by the Ministry of Agriculture, Food and Fisheries at Lowestoft.

Inland of the power stations, to the west and north, is an area of grazing marshes which is, botanically, the best in Suffolk. The SWT is undertaking a five-year management plan to get them back into condition. Cattle are now grazing there and eventually the public will be allowed limited access.

THORPENESS TO SIZEWELL

WOODPECKER

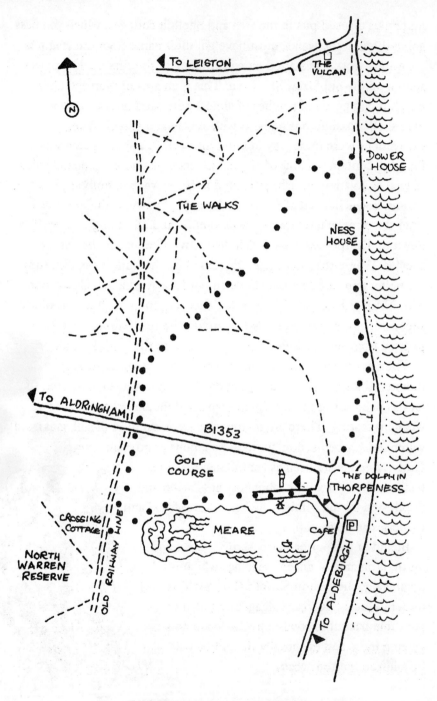

N

TO LEISTON

THE VULCAN

THE WALKS

DOWER HOUSE

NESS HOUSE

TO ALDRINGHAM

B1353

GOLF COURSE

THE DOLPHIN THORPENESS

CROSSING COTTAGE

MEARE

CAFE

P

NORTH WARREN RESERVE

OLD RAILWAY LINE

TO ALDEBURGH

THORPENESS TO SIZEWELL

The Dolphin, Thorpeness. Spacious pleasant pub in keeping with the area. Short but appetising bar menu, eg large home-baked baguettes with various fillings and toasted. £2.50. Dogs and children welcome. Large garden at side. Tel: 01728-452681.

The Vulcan Arms, Sizewell. Much nicer inside than it looks from the outside. Low-ceilinged bar divided up like an old stables. Garden. Menu includes things with chips, sandwiches and jacket potatoes. Well-behaved dogs and children welcome. Tel: 01728-830748.

Sizewell 'T', Beach Road, Sizewell Gap. Pleasant little pre-fab café on the dunes behind the beach. Breakfasts, coffee, tea, lunches, fish and chips to take away. Closed in winter.

Gallery Coffee Shop, next to the car park and opposite the entrance to Thorpeness Meare. Coffee, lunches (licenced). All day menu include fish and chips, burgers, soup and salads, take-aways. Open 9.30am-dusk. Also a craft and gift shop. Tel: 01728-831108.

Meare shop, on the Meare-side, Thorpeness. Teas, lunches, homemade cakes and soup. Open daily March-October, Tue-Sat October-February.

LOCAL INTEREST

The Mill, Heritage Coast Centre. The post mill moved from Aldringham in 1921 to pump water for the holiday village.

The House in the Clouds. The old water tower disguised as a house, now a holiday home.

Rowing boats on the Meare for hire.

Sizewell Visitor Centre, just north of the walk. Exhibition all about generating electricity, how nuclear power stations work, safety, environmental and ecological aspects of nuclear power. Lots of inveractive exhibits and gizmos – quite fun. Along the dunes you can view the reinstated dune and beach flora as it grows and establishes itself. Easy access for disabled people. Open daily, except Christmas and New Year holidays, 10am-4pm. Admission free. Tel: 01728-642139.

Aldringham Craft Market (see page 65).
Long Shop Museum, Leiston (see page 47).

THE WALK

An easy walk on heathland, woodland and along sandy cliffs with a
continual sea view. On the old railway line you will find tree lupins,
hawthorns, honeysuckle, briony, pear trees in season, to mention a few.

TRANSPORT

Park: opposite Thorpness Meare, free. Map ref: 473595, Pathfinder 1009.

4½ MILE WALK

Cross into the Meare enclosure and follow round to the right. Exit by
the gate opposite the houses. Cross onto a small green at the end of
which you turn left onto a footpath signed to Heritage Coast Centre
over the golf club drive and down through some gorse bushes. The
track follows the edge of the golf course on your right. After passing
Meare Cottage on the right, you come to an old level crossing gate and
the Crossing Cottage, turn right onto the disused railway track. When
you reach the road, cross over onto a continuation of the track to the
right of the white cottage. Shortly after this, where the concrete track
turns to dust, take the fork to the right. Where this track divides, take
either branch, they join up again a short distance ahead. At the next
fork, Corporals Belts, continue straight until you come to a path to the
right that bends slightly back on itself. Take this and, after a short
distance through the pine trees, in front of the Dower House, there is
a fence with a yellow waymark to the left. Follow this to the cliff top
and turn right. You can follow this path all the way back to the car park
in Thorpeness. Alternatively, before you get to the village – the path
by now is nearly down at beach level – you will find two or three paths
leading up the cliff onto Thorpeness Common, where you turn left
towards the houses on the outskirts of Thorpeness and wander back
through the village on any road you like.

NORTH WARREN TO ALDRINGHAM

7

NORTH WARREN is a RSPB reserve, and has long been an area of rabbit-grazed grassy heath. Once ploughed, its soil proved to be so impoverished, it was, thankfully, allowed to revert to heath where now the rabbits are again doing their best to keep it that way. Rabbits are essential for this type of area which attracts the stone curlew and wheatear. Woodpeckers love its plentiful supply of ants. As well as grassy heath, this gem of a reserve provides coastal grazing marshes with reed beds, deciduous woodland, alder carr, fen and the Hundred river.

In 1959, fire destroyed 90% of the heather, and the bracken took over – bracken's deep root system is not easily damaged by fire. The warden arrived in 1990 and began trying to reinstate the heath with heather seed collected from Dunwich. The acid heath and lichen areas are very scarce habitat and the warden is trying to increase this, adding a flock of sheep, owned by Suffolk Wildlife Trust, to help the rabbits with the grazing. The result is a good-looking sward which has attracted three pairs of woodlarks, one of Britain's rarest breeding birds. Ragwort tends to present problems; the only things to graze on it effectively being cinnebar moth caterpilllars and Beulah sheep. The former rely on the wind to blow them from colony to colony of ragwort – not a problem in East Suffolk! A few of the latter have been supplied and are doing a good job.

The reed beds had been neglected since commercial cutting stopped in 1955. Invaded by scrub, they had dried out. A lot of work has since gone into restoring them and the fen area. The reeds have rapidly recolonised and many species of flowers and birds have returned.

The 1987 storms did a favour to the woodlarks by creating clearings, thus providing suitable habitat for breeding, and so they have returned.

March mornings are a good time to hear them; April mornings for nightingales. Foreign visitors are common here and the very exotic South European Bee Eaters, which winter in Africa, return regularly.

North Warren abuts another small SWT reserve, The Haven, which occupies a small site either side of the Aldeburgh to Thorpeness road. The River Hundred, now a mere stream, enters the sea through a culvert at The Haven. On the landward side of the road among marshy grass and scrub, grow adder's tongue ferns and southern marsh orchids. On the sand of the beach side are some rarities such as clustered and suffocated clover, bur medick and sand catchfly – the shingle is covered in sea pea.

Aldringham, a tiny straggle of a village just outside Leiston, is mentioned in Domesday as part of the manor which included Thorpe and Leiston. It mentions sheep, bees, cattle and pigs – all animals that were kept on 'waste' or heathland. It shows a considerable decrease in the number of pigs over 20 years, suggesting a great degree of woodland clearance: pigs needed woods.

Belonging to the Abbot of Leiston in the 13th century, Leiston, Sizewell and Aldringham commons formed a complex that contained a vast rabbit warren. However, although the rabbits colonised the commons, the commoners were not at liberty to help themselves. If they were caught doing so in the time of George III, they could be transported for seven years. Rabbits graze very methodically and very close to the ground, leaving it almost bare in patches near their burrows. The usefulness of rabbits to maturing grassy heath is in cutting down tall plants, allowing the low growing ones the light and space to survive. They happily chomp through seedling gorse, bramble, birch and pine. They are particularly fond of heather and harebell, unfortunately, and – equally unfortunately – will only eat bracken if they are desperate. Rabbits are prey to foxes, stoats, and weasels, so these are attracted to heathland that supports rabbits. All of these animals will commandeer rabbit burrows and squat there.

Many of the tracks and paths that criss-crossed Aldringham common to Leiston and Sizewell, kept clear by centuries of daily use, seem rather neglected now, or swallowed up by the golf course. The now dismantled railway that ran between Aldeburgh and Leiston from 1860 to 1966 has recently been opened as a permissable footpath, and some unusual plants for the area can be found along its course – chalk-loving plants which are thought to grow on the old calcareous materials imported for use in building the railway.

WHERE TO EAT

The Parrot and Punchbowl, Aldringham crossroads. 16th-century beamed pub with bar, snug and dining room. Good selection of bar snacks available. Dogs allowed in snug. Tel: 01728-830221.

LOCAL INTEREST

Aldringham Craft Market, opposite the pub. One of the most interesting gift shops around. Tremendous range of British, particularly East Anglian, products. Good quality and prices. Aim to encourage young talented craftsmen and artists. Frequent exhibitions. Also houses a tiny coffee shop with homemade cakes, tea coffee and soft drinks. Tables spill out onto grass quadrangle in good weather. Open all year, Mon-Sat 10am-5.30pm. Sun 10am-12noon and 2-5.30pm, but check during autumn and winter. Tel: 01728-830397.

St ANDREWS CHURCH
ALDRINGHAM.

NORTH WARREN TO ALDRINGHAM

Long Shop Museum, Main St, Leiston (see page 47).
Sizewell Visitor Centre (see page 61).

THE WALKS

All these walks go through very attractive and varied countryside –
grass heathland, fen, woodland and heath. In May, you will find
bluebells and tree lupins amongst the gorse of the grassy heath, and
kingcups and marsh orchids in the fen; later on, purple heather and
orange-berried rowan trees. The short walk is easy going, the others
involve some climbing. Stout shoes are advisable.

TRANSPORT

Park: Limited parking at the entrance to North Warren nature
reserve. Turn right off the Leiston Road (from Aldeburgh) at the
footpath sign to Thorpeness, between two houses. Map ref: 455588,
Pathfinder 1009. You can also start from Aldringham church where
there is a large car park. Map ref: 452603, or from The Parrot and
Punchbowl pub.
Buses: Regular service from Saxmundham and Aldeburgh.

6 MILE WALK

From the entrance to North Warren, take the broad track straight
ahead through grassy heath. Continue on the path as it leads through
woods and bears to the left, passing part of Thorpeness Meare on the
right. On leaving the nature reserve, pass the old level crossing gate
and the keeper's cottage on your left and continue along the path
following the line of the dismantled railway until you get to the B1353
road. Cross and continue on the concreted path to the right of the
white cottage. When the track forks, keep straight ahead until you
reach a dismantled railway bridge where you turn left and take the
broad path across the golf course. This track eventually leads through
some trees onto a white gravel path where you turn left and walk
alongside the 15th hole, opposite which you turn right onto the path

through the bracken. This path curves round the top of the golf course. When you get to a T-junction, turn left and almost immediately right – the path still meanders through bracken but is swinging more to the left towards the road. It passes through a clump of gorse bushes and emerges in a clearing by the road (where you can park if you want to start the walk from here). Cross the road, taking the footpath through the trees onto the track by the almshouses, turn right to the church and take the footpath down through the very pretty churchyard which is a wildlife sanctuary. Follow the path round to the left of the charming 12th-century church, then diagonally right down to a gate in the corner and onto a footpath straight ahead. When you come to some mangy Scots pines on a rise to your left, you can see the village of Aldringham ahead. Follow the track down to the road and turn right. The Parrot and Punchbowl is on the left at the crossroads, about 200 yards ahead.

WOODLARK

On leaving Aldringham, go straight over the crossroads onto the B1353, towards Thorpeness, and after about 150 yards, take a path to the right beside an old corrugated iron barn. This brings you back to the track you arrived on, by the old schoolhouse. Turn left and follow the fenced path to the churchyard where you turn left up the sunken lane to the almshouses. Enter the churchyard by the main gate and turn immediately left, following the hedge along the top of the churchyard and into the field. The path now follows the left-hand edge of three fields, downhill. At the far side of the third field, don't follow the track into the next field, but turn left and a short distance along you will find a shallow stile in the hedge. Cross this and climb the bank to the next field. Turn right and follow the side of the field until you come to a barn with a pig weather vane and a three-way

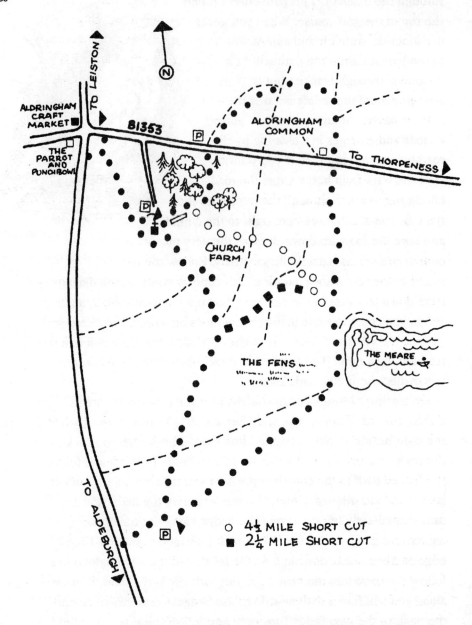

NORTH WARREN TO ALDRINGHAM

footpath sign. Carry on straight ahead up the track and across the next junction where you will find yourself on a narrow path by a lilac hedge that leads down to the Fen. Continue straight ahead, through a fence, onto a wooden boardwalk across the fen and the River Hundred. This leads to a heathland track which comes to a crossroads of paths with a wooden seat. Take the path straight ahead and back to the car.

4½ MILE WALK

Starting from the entrance to North Warren, you take the same route as for the six-mile walk as far as the old level crossing where, instead of continuing straight on, you turn left following the yellow waymarked path as it winds through birch, oak and willow scrub. On leaving the wood, follow the track towards Fen Cottage and, just before reaching it, turn right across a washing green, in front of a garage, and take the stile to the field. Turn left and, as you get to the top of the rise, you should see the footpath sign halfway along the hedge at the far side of the field – aim for it. Across the stile, the path goes through a patch of gorse and reaches the surfaced track. Cross straight over and down the track through Church Farm. Aim for the row of brick cottages, Ogilvie Almshouses, and the church. The walk now continues as for the six-mile walk to Aldringham and back again to the car park at North Warren.

2¼ MILE WALK

Again, set out from the North Warren entrance as for the other two walks, as far as the old level crossing. Here you turn left as for the 4½ mile walk, but when you get to Fen Cottage, keep straight on past the cottage and up a rise between gorse and brambles, with a good view over the fen to your left. Ignore the footpath sign to the left and carry straight on to a surfaced track where you turn left onto the signposted upper path. When this bends to the right by Bird's Farm, take the left fork under the trees and down the narrow path beside the lilac hedge, and continue across the fen, as for the previous walk.

NORTH WARREN TO ALDRINGHAM

8

TUNSTALL FOREST, SNAPE AND BLAXHALL HEATH

A port since Roman times, it is thought that the first settlement of Snape was down by the river, and that the population expanded in the 12th and 13th centuries when the village moved uphill to the higher ground. The nature of the area in the past is reflected in the name of a local pub – The Plough and Sail. Farmers ploughed and harvested crops which they then took down river in their own sailing barges. Further down the river at Iken there were coal yards which imported coal in schooners from Newcastle.

The Romans settled Yarn Hill at Iken, then an island, and Boudicca led the Iceni tribes, who had previously settled the area, in battles against them. There is plenty of evidence of both Roman and Iron Age settlement in the Alde Valley, and Iron Age Brits settled around Snape Common. The Snape area was invaded and settled by all the same incomers as settled the other estuaries and some of the place names are thought to reflect their influence; Carnser, old Frisian for causeway, Snape itself and Iken, Icanhoe – a headland. St Botolph's church is named for the 7th-century monk who built a model monastery in what was described at the time as 'a dismal Godforsaken place, surrounded by swamps.' Five hundred or so years ago the church was on an island and could only be reached on foot at low tide. Much of the area is now covered by flourishing arable land reclaimed from marsh and heath; and is home to shelduck, redshank, heron and avocet who live among the sea purslane, glasswort, sea aster and arrow-grass along the river.

In 1862 an Anglo Saxon ship was discovered, of the same period though not as important as Sutton Hoo. The burial site is either

side of the A1094 Aldeburgh Road, but nothing can be seen of it.
The fields have long since been levelled and crops grown on them.
Excavation in 1985 turned up a further boat, and the skeleton of a man
with a sword, and auburn hair – the acid sandy soil had preserved the
remains very well.

Probably the most famous landmark in the area is Snape Maltings
which Newson Garrett started to build in 1846, at the same time as he
and his brother Richard joined the pressure group to extend the East
Suffolk railway to Leiston and Aldeburgh. Newson got a branch line to
Snape for goods only. Prior to this, many goods travelled up and down
the river by barge, a journey of some 12 miles to the sea which is only
four miles as the crow flies. The railway also served other interests in
Snape. It carried coal, building materials and agricultural products,
specially sugar beet, which was introduced to the area in 1911 by the
then landlord of the Crown Inn. The Maltings operated continuously
for 120 years, the barley used being locally grown until demand
outgrew supply and it had to be imported. The malt was used for
various beers, Guinness and Ovaltine. The Maltings finally closed in
1965 when new malting techniques demanded more modern
buildings. The Aldeburgh Festival Committee converted the large

'DISTANT VIEW OF
SNAPE MALTINGS
FROM THE WARREN'

TUNSTALL FOREST, SNAPE AND BLAXHALL HEATH

malthouse into a concert hall which was burnt down in 1969 but quickly rebuilt and re-opened in 1970.

Tunstall Forest and Blaxhall Heath are areas of sandy acid soil on crag and Chillesford clays. Before 1920, most of the area was heathland, mainly used for grazing. When the Forestry Commission took over the land, they eradicated the rabbits, erected rabbit-proof fencing and ploughed and planted acres of pine. They tried oaks on some old arable land but this was not successful. Conifers take about 60 years to reach maturity and out of 2,000 per acre planted, only 150 will last the course. There are some natural losses but its mostly a question of the way trees are 'farmed'. At 16-20 years old they are 'brashed', that is all branches below six foot are removed. Then the trees are thinned out about every four years. The trees in Tunstall had just reached maturity when they were practically clear-felled by the 1987 hurricane. Now the regeneration of the forest is being done in a more sympathetic way, taking care to create a diversity of habitat for a variety of wildlife. There are fallow and roe deer, hares and rabbits, stoats and weasels, and even red squirrels.

Blaxhall Heath, in Tunstall Forest, is managed as a mosaic of heather and other plants, providing considerable areas of heather. With more resources, more heather could be maintained but bracken needs to be cut three or four times a year for four years to clear it. Pine and birch scrub is grubbed out by hand by volunteer working parties. But, as birch stops the bracken growing, remove the birch and the bracken has a clear field. The working parties often burn bracken and other rubbish. You can sometimes tell where they have done this because a patch of rose bay willow herb – fireweed – has grown up.

Two interesting features on the common are an iron age burial site and

BRACKEN

the gipsy pit. The burial mound was opened in the 1800's and some artifacts removed. It was then closed again as they hadn't the technology to remove any more without doing damage.

The gipsy pit is a hollow where gipsies once parked their caravans. Today, it is filled with trees and bracken, but ten years ago, it was a grassy hollow. The grass was worn away by motor cycles and four-track vehicles using it as a race track. The disappearance of the grass enabled the bracken to take over. The whole process was not helped by Americans from the nearby base having parties in it, leaving their bottles behind, now hidden under a pile of wood chips – a result of Forestry Commission activity.

In the anti-glider trench, from the second World War, south of the Snape Road, you can get a good idea of the soil profile. There is 20cm of nutritious top soil, about 30-45 cm of grey podsol, leached of all nutrients; then another nutrient layer on top of the shelly sandy glacial drift. The holes you can see are made by solitary bees and wasps and there are webs of funnel web spiders in the heather. Nightjars nest on the ground and, in July, the males 'churr' in the tall pines at night. Yellow-hammers, green woodpeckers and cross bills inhabit the heath, while skylarks and kestrels roam the farmland.

WHERE TO EAT

The Crown Inn, Snape. Very attractive old smugglers inn. Has a bar completely filled by a large semicircular old high-backed settle facing the fire. Nice dining room. Large garden in open country at back. Children over 14 welcome if eating, but no dogs. Tel: 01728-688324.
The Golden Key. Very pleasant beamed bar with a tiled floor, round tables and large open fire. Gravel terrace with tables at front. Lots of steaks etc, some vegetarian options. Egon Ronay recommended. Children allowed if eating. Dogs welcome. Tel: 01728-688510.
The Plough And Sail. Long, narrow bar at front with log fire. Dining room at back, large paved patio garden, with giant chess game. Interesting menu. Children and dogs welcome. Tel: 01728-688413.

The Ship, Blaxhall village. The name may be a corruption of Sheep since it's rather a long way from any water. Long L-shaped bar. Pleasant sunny dining room, and terrace in front. Lunch every day except Mondays includes a vegetarian dish. Large appetizing portions. No dogs. Tel: 01728-688316.

Fish and chip shop, Snape. On the main road just past The Crown. Open Tue, Thu and Sat midday, Wed and Fri eves.

Granary Tea Shop, Snape Maltings. Tea, coffee, homemade cakes and savouries available daily, all year.

LOCAL INTEREST

Snape Maltings. Open daily, 10am-6pm (-5pm in winter). Tel: 01728-688303/5. The complex incorporates shops selling craft gifts, plants, kitchenware, gourmet foods, clothes, books and music. Art gallery with original paintings by local artists. There is also a Victorian bird collection. **River trips** on the Alde estuary. Easter-October, 1hr trips, £3 adults, £2.50 children. New for 1995, sail on the old barge Ethel Ada from **Snape Quay.** Tel: 01473-822054, or enquire at the Maltings office. Self-catering accommodation. Two cottages and a flat. Send an sae to Snape Maltings, IP17 1SR for details.

THE WALKS

Both walks are fairly easy, with fine views over the Alde estuary (pity about the pylons!). The first is an interesting walk following a causeway across reed beds, marsh and wet meadows. The second walk is almost entirely on the flat through farmland and Tunstall Forest.

TRANSPORT

Park: Snape Maltings car park. Map ref: 392573, Pathfinder 1008.

Buses: Regular service from Woodbridge. Villager service, also stops in Blaxhall occasionally. Tel: 01728-604347.

Turn right out of the Maltings complex, cross Snape bridge and take
the footpath marked to the right along the river bank (dogs on lead).
After following the river for some way, the path enters a small wood
and turns left where it broadens out amongst the gorse, bracken,
brambles and oaks. After about ¼ of a mile, take the clearly marked
footpath to the left along the Canser (causeway) – do not follow Coastal
Path sign. At the end of the path, turn sharp right, following a yellow
waymark, to the road where you turn right again, for a short distance.
Ignore the first track to your left opposite Fir Tree House and take
the second one, opposite the entrance to The Cloisters. There is a
bridleway sign, fallen over and buried in the hedge, but a sign up a tree
points to Belle Vue House. Follow this track and keep straight on past
a left-hand fork, with playing fields behind the hedge on your right.
You come to another left-hand fork which again you ignore, continuing
straight ahead on the path which has narrowed. The path continues
through arable fields to the road. Across this, it continues along the
edge of what remains of Snape Common. (If you have time, Snape
Church is a delightful small, simple church.) When you reach the next
road, turn very sharply left down Wadd Lane, leaving a garage on your
right. After following this bracken-lined road for about ¼ mile, you
come to a footpath leading off to the left through a small spinney with
brambles and gorse. Cross the stile and follow the path across the field
towards a pink cottage on the far side. Here you cross Gromford Lane
and follow the 'No through road' lane for about ¼ mile. When you pass
the last cottage (which appears to run an old car yard), you take the
footpath ahead along the edge of a small conifer spinney. At the end,
the path turns left and follows the edge of a field, separated from it by
a low wire netting fence, and comes out further down Gromford Lane,
by a house called The Bents. Turn right onto the road for a mere 20
yards or so, then turn right onto the footpath. Follow this (yellow
waymark) and just before the end of the field take the path signed to
the left and cross towards the farm buildings; follow the right side of

TUNSTALL FOREST, SNAPE AND BLAXHALL HEATH

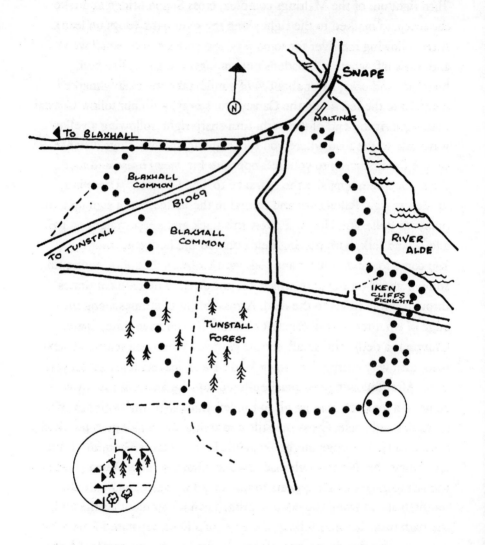

TUNSTALL FOREST, SNAPE AND BLAXHALL HEATH

the field to the wooden footpath sign between two buildings. Take the broad farm track straight ahead past Abbey Farmhouse to the road where you turn right towards the Maltings, a short distance away.

5½ MILE WALK

Take the footpath from the far right-hand corner of the car park behind the Britten-Pears School, past the fence and the chestnut trees, and turn right between two hedges. After a short distance, turn left across the marshes, there is a boardwalk across the swampy bit. The track continues through an area of newly planted trees, with the river away to your left. Follow the path through Iken Cliff picnic site and into the trees at the far side. At the end of this narrow path, you come onto a broad sandy track; take the path that curves to the left down towards the river, to the left of the cottage. The path ahead lies along a beach and may not be passable at some high tides, in which case take the upper right-hand path before you reach the cottage. From the beach turn right at a signpost and up some steps to the top of the cliff. You come to a T-junction; the path from the right is the one you'd have taken at high tide. At the road, where there is a sign pointing the way you've come, turn right for a short distance then over a stile on the left into a field. The path skirts two sides of this field, past a large corrugated iron building and over a stile, where you turn left to the next signpost by a pumping station at the head of a small reservoir. Turn sharply right here, keeping the reservoir on your right and passing a Dutch barn on your left. At the top of this field, turn left alongside some pine woods. At the next signpost, turn right, still following the edge of the pine woods. The pines give way to birches and at the end of the birches is another signpost. Turn right here and immediately left, then again right at the far side of a small belt of pines. At the end of the pines, you come to a road; cross it diagonally to your right and onto a broad stony track into Tunstall Forest. Follow this path as far as a cottage and dovecote behind a fence on your left, then a clearing with cross tracks. Turn right here and after about 100 yards, fork left onto a grass track (yellow waymark). Follow signs straight ahead and over another track crossing yours at an angle. When you get to a road, cross straight over into a wood. At a cluster of tall Scots pines, take the track to the left between some posts. Cross over the road and straight ahead onto Blaxhall Common and a broad sandy bridleway through heathland. After about ½ mile, you come to cross tracks with a Blaxhall Parish Council sign to the right. Turn right here (NNE), and when you get to a clearing with a steep dip on the right, take the narrow path straight ahead, downhill. It ends at a road where you turn right, and after about ½ mile on this quiet road, you join the main road to Snape. This is busy but you only follow it for about 150 yards before you get to a triangle of grass at another road junction. At the far side of the grass, you'll see the footpath sign. Follow this and at the end of the brick wall, turn left towards the concert hall and back to the car park.

IKEN CHURCH
FROM IKEN CLIFFS

TUNSTALL FOREST, SNAPE AND BLAXHALL HEATH

THORPE HYTHE TO SLAUGHDEN

9

UNTIL THE MID-16TH CENTURY, the port of Aldeburgh was at the mouth of the shallow Hundred river. Ships anchored in the lee of the hill on which the church stands. As the Middle Ages advanced, the river began to silt up so ships took to sailing up the deeper channel of the River Alde and tied up at Slaughden where they were sheltered by both the higher ground of Aldeburgh and by Orford Ness. Slaughden (*Slog-dene*, meaning muddy river) quickly developed into a busy port with ship-building yards and warehouses holding goods for export and import. Fish, salt and local bricks were exported and coal and wine, amongst other things, imported. The port employed hundreds of men, both on the ships and on the quayside.

Aldeburgh had long been a busy and important fishing port, and as salt was needed to pack and preserve the fish, a salt industry flourished in the 16th century, salt pans having been established here about 400 years previously. The town was thriving and the population expanding when, in 1562, famine struck. The corn crop was struck by blight, making it inedible, but the appearance of a great crop of sea peas on the shingle near Orford is said to have saved the town from starvation. At this time the sea was making serious inroads on the town. A dozen or more houses were destroyed in one storm and in 1591, 20 feet of land was lost in one tide. During the next two centuries, the sea continued to eat away at the town, and by the end of the 18th century, much of the northern end had completely vanished. People began leaving Aldeburgh and its fortunes declined.

Down at the Slaughden end, ships were still fishing and trading, although a lot of the shipping trade had moved to the Thames when larger ships found the Alde too shallow. In the mid 1800s, there were plans to make an opening to the sea at Slaughden to create a harbour, but they came to nothing. A few years later the port declined.

Towards the end of the century, shingle was being repeatedly thrown up around the buildings at high tides and sea water is said to have entered the pub by the back door and exited through the front. Finally, at the beginning of this century, all traces of Slaughden were washed away. A shepherd's house that was south east of the Martello tower in 1900 now lies in ruins on the sea bed about quarter of a mile off-shore. The tower, when built in 1815, had a road and a quite extensive green between it and the sea.

In the early 1900s, Aldeburgh became a flourishing seaside town with a railway (closed in 1969), a golf course and the country's first woman mayor, Elizabeth Garrett-Anderson, one of the talented daughters of Newson Garrett. The first woman doctor in Britain, she founded a hospital for women in St. Pancras, and her sister Millicent Garrett Fawcett was a prominent suffragette.

Recently there were 25-locally built boats based at Aldeburgh, fishing from Sizewell to Orford Ness. They bring fish in daily – weather permitting – and some is sold from huts on the beach.

WHERE TO EAT

Aldeburgh is full of pubs, restaurants and cafés. Unless you must eat at a table with cutlery and plates, you could do worse than visit the excellent fish and chip shop at the Slaughden end of the High Street. Open Tue-Sat 11.45am-1.45pm. Thur-Sat evenings 5-9 pm, Tue to 8 pm.

LOCAL INTEREST

The Martello Tower is the largest and most northerly of a string of such towers built along the coast for defence during the

SEA PEA

THORPE HYTHE TO SLAUGHDEN

Napoleonic wars. It had been the intention to fill the moat by piping water from the river, but it has never had water in it. There was originally a drawbridge and the moat encircled the tower which was some distance from the sea. About 130 feet of shore disappeared from in front of the tower over about 45 years around the turn of the century. It now belongs to the Landmark Trust and is let out as a holiday home.

Moot Hall Museum and Town Hall. Built 1520-1540. Open Easter-October, April and May weekends 2.30-5pm, June and September daily 2.30-5pm, July and August daily 10.30am-12.30pm and 2.30-5pm. Admission 35p, children free.

Aldeburgh church. A large pleasant church with three aisles. It contains the Britten Memorial window, designed by John Piper and depicting three of Britten's operas in vivid colours.

Hazelwood Marshes, SWT nature reserve. Park in the roadside car park and walk into the reserve by the Sailors Path, that goes all the way to Snape. There is a hide on the river at Ham Creek. The entrance is on the right approaching Aldeburgh, just a short distance after the town sign.

Haven Nature Reserve. Either side of the Aldeburgh to Thorpeness road. Just before you reach the derelict Sluice Cottage; car park on the right. At the end of the car park, the reserve begins. There are no notices.

The Walled Garden, Benhall. A lovely nursery selling some unusual plants in a large, old walled garden. From the south, turn left off the A12 just before the turning to Aldeburgh. It is signposted. Closed Mon.

THE WALK

This walk goes around the outskirts of Aldeburgh, taking in the sites of its two old medieval harbours. An easy walk, it can be done in two stages – you can walk across the marshes to Slaughden and back, or go north towards Thorpe Hythe, round the church, and back through the Victorian part of the high town; this would also provide an opportunity to descend the Town Steps and wander around the streets of the lower town.

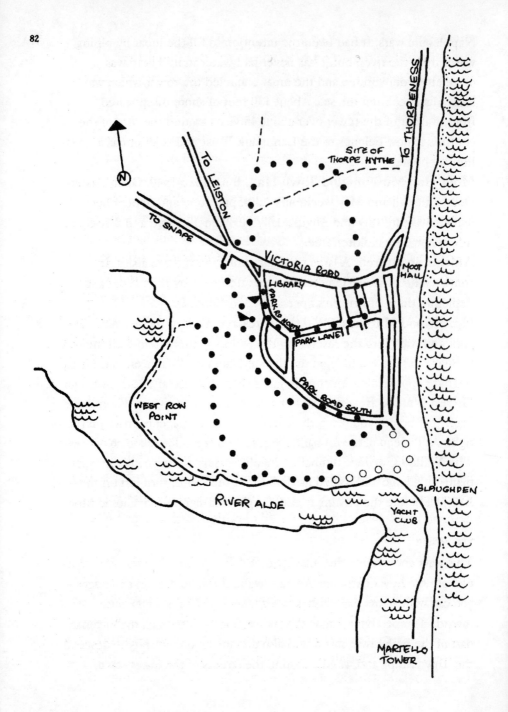

THORPE HYTHE TO SLAUGHDEN

TRANSPORT

Park: in road by the library. Map ref: 460569 Pathfinder 1009 .
Buses: regular services from Woodbridge, Saxmundham and Leiston.

4½ MILE WALK

Go past the library and through the gates into the private road of large
houses, some of which were built by Newson Garrett for his six
children. Just before you reach Priors Hill Road, turn right onto an
asphalt path leading to the tennis club. You come to a cross tracks and,
ahead, a gate onto a path leading through some allotments – follow
this FP sign to West Low Point. You cross three or four foot bridges
over drainage ditches through the marshes. Continue to a signpost.
If the weather is fine and warm, you may like to continue ahead and
follow the loop of the river wall. This will add about one and a half
miles to the walk. Otherwise, turn left here and follow the footpath,
keeping the ditch on your right all the way to the flood wall. Turn left
at the wall or climb onto it and turn left along it. From here, you can
see how the marshes grade into drier land, where the hawthorns and
willows start and the ground rises very slightly. There are saltings to the
right of the wall and reeds and lagoons to the left. This wall has been
strengthened in places by concrete blocks, and you can appreciate
how much energy is in the water as it bashes against the concrete, in
contrast with the way it is dissipated on the nearby saltings. Just after
the concrete section, there are some steps down to the left. You can
descend here, cross a ditch and head towards the town. Don't follow
the gravelly track where it forks, but branch off on the grassy path to
the right. When you come to Park Road, turn right and then left at the
High Road for shops, etc. Rather than leave the river wall, you could
continue on it until it meets the sea wall just by the yacht club. Turn
left along the sea wall and walk into Aldeburgh. Turn left into Park
Road and walk up it, past a cream-washed, pebble dash primary
school, and fork left onto a broad, sandy track, with marsh on the left
and houses and gardens rising up on the right. Continue along this

THORPE HYTHE TO SLAUGHDEN

path, past the turning where you joined it, and across the recreation
ground. Just before you reach the road, there are some basic but
welcome public toilets. At the road, turn right and just a few yards
along on your left, turn onto the footpath. Cross the road leading into
the new estate; the footpath continues on the other side. When you
come to the caravan park, keep straight on. This is the route of the old
railway. At the end of the houses, the permissive footpath continues
ahead along the old railway track. Instead of following this interesting-
looking track, turn right into the caravan park and continue through it
to the toilet block, where you turn right behind it and go through a
gate on the left. Cross the road and take the narrow footpath between
tall hedges, going up to the church. Go through the gate into the
churchyard and round to the left of the church. Cross the main road
(Victoria Road) into Church Walk. This brings you out onto the
Terrace at the top of Town Steps. Turn right into Park Lane. Go
straight over Alde Lane and continue ahead on the unmade road to
Park Road, in front of the Victorian water tower. Turn right and follow
the road back to your car.

THE STEPS
ALDEBURGH.

THORPE HYTHE TO SLAUGHDEN

ORFORD

10

THE SMALL FISHING and farming settlement of Orford became an important port after the castle and church were built in the 12th century. The castle was started in 1165 by Henry II; quays were built for unloading construction materials and marshes around the castle were 'inned' to create farmland on which enough food could be grown to feed the soldiers garrisoned at the castle. At this time, Orford was on the coast, with the sea reaching up to what is now Broad Street.

In later medieval times, the population reached 1,000, all of whom could easily fit into St. Bartholomew's church – all that remains of this first church are the ruined chancel arcades. The present church has been re-built and restored over the centuries. A good deal of septaria, the local mudstone, was used in the tower; as it's not very durable, it may have been responsible for the collapse of the tower in 1830. Several other local church towers containing septaria have collapsed, but the castle keep seems to have held up well. Concerts are sometimes held in the church, as part of the Aldeburgh Festival, and Britten's operas *Noyes Fludde* and *Curlew River* were premiered here.

Two very important areas of Orford are Havergate Island and Orford Ness. Havergate Island is thought to have been formed during the 16th and 17th centuries as the shingle spit moved south, isolating Orford from the sea. It is about two miles long and made up of shingle, saltmarsh and lagoons. It is very bleak and treeless, though there is some tamarisk, gorse and elder which offers cover to hares. Sea purslane and sea lavender flourish on the saltmarsh and sea pea and English stonecrop on the shingle beach. In the middle of the last century, a family lived there, surviving on rabbits, hares, wild fowl and the eggs of plovers and terns. They caught fish and grew vegetables and chickens. Up until 1939, sheep and cattle were ferried over from the mainland for summer grazing.

During the war, the island was used for target practice and a stray shell destroyed a sluice, creating lagoons with islands, which provided an ideal breeding ground for avocets. Discovering this, the RSPB bought the island in 1947 and developed the nature reserve. There is still no fresh water nor mains electricity, and the resident warden has to have water shipped in, and runs a wind generator to provide electric light. Havergate now has the largest breeding colony of avocets in Britain, as well as many other species of birds. There are hides overlooking all the lagoons, and basic toilets for visitors. Visiting is restricted to certain times of the year.

Orford Ness is the largest vegetated shingle spit in Europe, containing nationally rare shingle heath plant communities, and is an important breeding ground for a number of birds, notably oyster-catchers. There are 112 identified species of lichen, and seals can sometimes be seen swimming in the Ore.

The growth of Orford Ness has always been erratic and is constantly being re-shaped by the elements. In the hard winters of 1944-5 and 1946-7, large ice floes caused by snow falling on the mud flats at Iken, were brought down to Orford by the tide, eventually cutting the island off from the mainland. The floods in January 1953 drowned several hundred sheep grazing on Orford Ness, and Havergate Island all but disappeared. The water reached almost to the top of Quay Street and the water level at the Jolly Sailor is marked by a brass strip on the fireplace.

Orford Ness was an experimental flying station during the First World War. German prisoners were put to work to drain marshes and build sea walls. In the mid-1920s, it was used as a testing range for guns and bombs. Turf was taken from the saltings and used to provide a sports field and lawns for the officers at Martlesham airfield. From the mid-1930s, radar was being developed at Orford Ness, and later, at Bawdsey by Sir Robert Watson Watt who stayed at the Crown and Castle. After the war, the isolated position of the Ness continued to be exploited for testing nuclear weapons. The pagoda-shaped buildings you can see were designed to collapse if an underground nuclear explosion was too large. Later on, the Cobra Mist radio surveillance system was opened to monitor Eastern bloc military radio communications. In the late 1970s, the military finished with Orford Ness. The Cobra masts were removed and thousands of bombs had to be dealt with. The BBC took over the Cobra site for the World Service.

WHERE TO EAT

Crown And Castle Hotel. A comfortable old hotel, Les Routiers recommended. Lunchtime bar snacks, evening meals, morning coffee, afternoon teas and breakfasts available. No dogs, children in lounge only. Tel: 01394-450205.

King's Head. Old beamed pub. Large, interesting menu, good helpings, well presented. Garden and car park. Open all day Saturdays. In Good Pub guide. Dogs allowed on a lead in the bar, children welcome in the restaurant. Tel: 01394-450271.

Jolly Sailor. Unspoilt traditional local pub with low ceilings, stone floors. Big grassy garden overlooks Gedgrave Marshes. Good value dishes; local fish and chips, steak pie, etc. No children under 14, well-behaved dogs allowed in middle bar. Tel: 01394-450243.

Butley Orford Oysterage, Market Hill. Started in the 1950's by the father of the present owner who farms the oysters in Butley Creek near his cottage. Great variety of fish dishes. Tel: 01394-450277.

Village store could provide ingredients for a very good picnic. Open Sundays 10am-1pm.

AVOCET

Old Warehouse tea room and art gallery, The Quay. Excellent homemade cakes and scones. Also does lunches. Licensed. Open all week, all year except February. Tel: 01394-450210.

LOCAL INTEREST

Orford Castle, Open daily April-October 10am-6pm, November-March 10am-4pm.

Boat Trips. One-hour trip round Havergate Island. Daily, weather permitting, April-September. £4 adult, £2 children (1994 prices). Tel: 01394-450637.

Four-hour trips up the Alde and down the Ore. All year. Food available on board, and bar. Goes at midday. £8 (1994 price). Evening dinner trips in summer. Book at Warehouse. Tel: 01831-698298.

On boat trips and reserve trips it is advisable to take binoculars, though they can be hired on Havergate Island.

Craft shop, next to King's Head, with a museum of undersea exploration conducted off Dunwich. Open daily 11am-5pm. Tel: 01394-450678.

Orford Museum opened 1994 behind the Crown and Castle. Moving sometime to another site behind the town hall.

Secondhand books sold in house in Quay Street – through garden – for Save The Children.

Lighthouse. The first coal-fired one built of wood in 1603 burnt down, as did several of its successors, if they were not destroyed by the sea first. Present one built in the 1700s, 99 foot high, electrified 1959.

Havergate Island Nature Reserve, RSPB. Limited access by boat from Orford Quay between March and September. Tickets from the warden, John Partridge, 30 Mundays Lane, Orford, IP12 2LX. Members £3, non-members £5. Enclose sae.

Orford Ness National Nature Reserve, belonging to English Nature. Unlimited access on foot only. No dogs, fires or camping allowed because of the fragile nature of the habitat.

Orford Ness National Trust Reserve. Ferry from Orford Quay. Opens June 1995. Small charge for visitors.

A level walk through arable land that was once heath, wet and drained marshland and the delightful streets of Orford. Part of the walk goes along the flood wall of the River Ore with views of Orford Ness.

TRANSPORT

Park: Pay and Display car park at end of Quay Street. Map ref: 424496, Pathfinder 1009. From Woodbridge take A1152, then B1078 to Orford. **Buses:** daily service Monday-Saturday and summer Sunday service.

3¹/₂ MILE WALK

Walk up Quay Street to Market Hill and enter the churchyard through the gates to the side of the King's Head. The footpath goes round the right-hand side of the church, round the back of the ruined chancel and to the wall at the far side of the graveyard. At the gate, turn right and follow the path along the wattle fence, the brick wall, and round to the left, continuing along this shady path to emerge on Rectory Road. Cross straight over – the footpath goes through the crop but it's clearly marked and well trodden. Turn right onto the road in front of the cottages. At the end of the very large field on your right, you come to a crossroads. Take the right turn and when the road forks, take the left, dead-end road to Raydon Hall. Just before you reach the Hall, there is a footpath sign to the right, over a stile; cross the field diagonally and over another stile and a small stream overhung by a chestnut tree. The narrow, shaded path leads to another stile, ivy clad, and then continues ahead through a crop field (well trodden). You come to a stile which leads you through a cottage garden and out onto a road where you turn left for a short distance. Just before an imposing brick gateway, topped with pineapples (stone ones), on your right, turn left into the broad, grassy track called Doctors' Drift – probably an old sheep or cattle drove before the marshes were drained. At the end of the drainage ditch, the path turns right, crosses a strip of marsh and goes up onto the river wall. Turn right towards Orford Quay and follow the path to

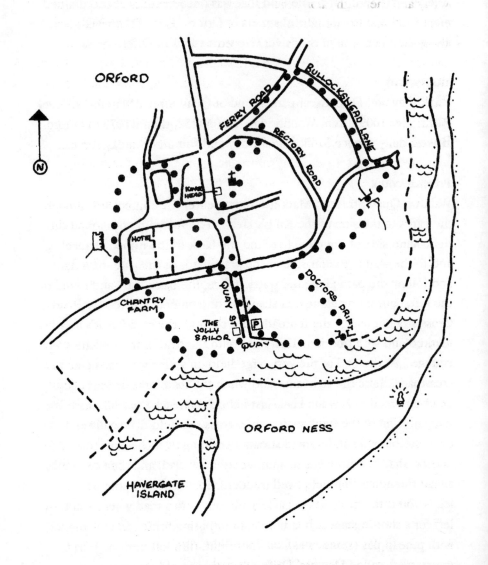

ORFORD

its end outside the Old Warehouse tea shop. Turn left down to the
Quay and then right alongside the river. The path goes up onto the
river wall; just before it bends to the left, turn right off the wall, cross
the bridge over a marshy ditch and reed bed into a field, and walk
towards the castle. The path goes through Chantry Farm yard and joins
the road. Follow it round to the castle, and take the sandy track up the
right side of the castle, which gives you a good view down over the
river. If you want to turn this into a longer walk, see below for extra
directions. Otherwise, turn right here between the houses and the
recreation ground. At the end turn right, again back to the centre of the
village – the new houses here are built on what was the site of the
medieval market. Instead of returning to the car park via Quay Street,
you can meander down any of the alleyways and side streets, all very
attractive routes.

To lengthen your walk – from Orford Castle, go left into Munday's
Lane, behind the fire station, and take the footpath through
Sudbourne Park. Sudbourne Hall, now demolished, was once the home
of Richard Wallace, provider of the Wallace Collection. Follow the
Friars' Walk to Chillesford, where you turn left onto the B1054 and left
again into Mill Lane (opposite the village shop). A footpath to the left
leads into the Seedlings; turn left past Carmens Wood, then left again
to Butley Low Corner. Turn right to the T-junction, then left towards
and over Burrow Hill, down to the Ferry. Cross on the ferry to
Gedgrave Cliffs and walk into Orford along Gedgrave Road. If an even
longer walk is appealing, turn right down Havergate or Chantry Drifts
and walk along the river to the Quay.

NB. To use the ferry, it is essential to phone the ferryman and arrange
with him to take you across (tel: 01394-410096). For other walks
around Orford, see the Suffolk County Council leaflet.

11

BUTLEY TO BOYTON

THERE IS EVIDENCE of a number of Roman and Saxon settlements in this area. In Butley a hoard of old broken bronze tools were found, thought to be a pile waiting to be melted down and re-fashioned by some itinerant Bronze Age smith. Suffolk having no natural deposits of tin or copper, people had to recycle imported goods at sites where there was plenty of wood for charcoal.

Burrow Hill was a very early settlement and Saxon burial ground. Excavations carried out in 1983 unearthed coffins containing bodies dated around 780AD and a small kiln from 830AD. Remnants of writing implements, window glass, textiles and food, suggested a literate people with high living standards. When gravel was being removed from the top of the hill to repair the roads in Butley, around 200 skeletons were found.

In the late 12th century, when Butley Priory was built, the river mouth stretched from around Boyton to Gedgrave cliffs. Barges brought stone up the river for building the priory, and the canons established a ferry to take them across the river to their fields on the other side. The present ferryman came across the medieval foundations when he was building the new jetties. Following the dissolution of the monasteries, the priory fell into decay and the 14th-century gatehouse was converted to a private residence in 1737. One of its owners, the Marquis of Donegal, is thought to have planted the quincunxes (the clumps) lining the road to Staverton Park. These are groups of five trees – four beeches and a pine. About nine or ten clumps survive in various states of decay. They are supposed to symbolise the five wounds of Christ, and the road was known as the Pilgrims' Way. Another theory is that they were planted in 1805 to commemorate the battle of Trafalgar. Others say that they were planted that way in an effort to grow straight pines for ships' masts. Rather distorted drawings of various ships have been discovered carved into the trees, which might possibly lend weight to either of the latter theories.

Staverton Thicks, in Staverton Park, is ancient woodland with some 400-year-old oaks, descendants of the original trees in the primeval forests that covered most of the county before the arrival of the early settlers. Evidence for their being continuous forest here is that there is no podsol – leached, inorganic soil – which would have developed had this ever been heathland. There are also species of lichen that only occur in places with continuous woodland cover. Roe and fallow deer live in the park, often seen crossing the road. A footpath goes through the Thicks from the B1084 to a bridleway leading to Wantisden Corner.

During the Middle Ages there was considerable shipping on the Butley river; corn was taken to Butley Mills for grinding, but after the dissolution trade and shipping slackened off. The shingle spit moved down south of the river mouth and gradually the upper reaches of the river began to silt up and reed beds grew across it, though barges still came up to the Mill as recently as 1914. The walling continued, with the 'inning' of the marshes, and the present course of the creek is probably a result of the final walling phase carried out by the Dutch in the 17th century. Boyton Marshes are being re-instated, and flooding started in August 1994. Abbey Farm, which contains the few remaining bits of Butley Priory, exported lupin seeds to Belgium at the turn of the century for dye-making.

Just before the creek discharges into the Ore, it passes Boyton Dock. It was from here, in the 18th century, that the very fine clay, found in a local field and suitable for making delftware, was exported to London, Holland and even America. Profits from the clay helped to support the Mary Warner almshouses in Boyton, and so, later, did the coprolites. The phosphate content of coprolite, and

BUTLEY TO BOYTON

SNOWDROPS

hence its commercial potential as an agricultural fertilizer, was discovered by Professor John Stevens Henslow in 1845 while staying in Felixstowe. The name coprolites comes from the Greek words for dung and stone because people believed it was fossilized dung. It is now believed that coprolite was probably formed when phosphates, from organic remains on the sea floor, were preciptated in mud. They were found amongst fossiliferous shelly crag, usually in a layer at the base of Red Crag deposits There were particularly extensive deposits on the Deben peninsular. At Boyton, they were dug from 1850 to 1957 and exported via Boyton Dock. James Fison exported over 2,000 tons from Bawdsey, Boyton, Woodbridge and Ipswich to King's Lynn.

When landowners became worried about the damage to their land, the coprolite was dug from trenches 20 feet apart. The top soil was removed and then carefully replaced afterwards – a bit like open cast coal mines today. There is now no trace of these trenches. In the 1880s cheap imports of phosphates started to arrive, mainly from the USA, and the local business declined.

At the head of Butley Creek is Chillesford, where the jaw bone of a whale was dug up in the old crag pit behind the church – it swam up the river when it was a tributary of the Rhine, so they say!

WHERE TO EAT

The Oyster, Butley. Simple, pleasant pub – scrubbed deal tables, copper pots and Victorian fireplaces. Small garden at back with dovecote and aviary. Food served daily except Sunday evenings. Variety of steaks, grills, pies and casseroles. Traditional bread pudding. Dogs welcome. Tel: 01349-450790.

The Bell, Boyton. 250-year-old pub with restaurant. Open all day. Garden. Dogs welcome. Tel: 01394-411710.

The Froize (The Friars, with a Suffolk accent or a thick pancake served by the friars of Butley, take your pick!), Chillesford. Cosy, low-ceilinged bar with a woodburner in a wide brick hearth and some interesting old wall clocks. Large garden at back. Food served daily.

Wide-ranging menu of basic but cheap dishes includes two vegetarian choices and old-fashioned puddings. Dogs welcome. Tel: 01394-450282. **Butley Pottery Tea Barn**, Mill Lane. Beautifully converted thatched barns with pottery, shop, gallery and tea room. Seats outside among ingenious scrap-metal sculptures. Drinks, homemade cakes and lunches, including vegetarian dishes, served all day. Open 10.30 am-5pm daily, April to September; Wed-Sun, October to March. Sometimes closed January. Tel: 01394-450785.

LOCAL INTEREST

Butley Ferry. To cross the creek to Gedgrave and Orford, ring the ferryman, preferably at weekends. He will cycle from his home to row you across. Tel: 01394-410096, Mr Rogers.
Staverton Thicks. Prehistoric woodland. Footpath through wood from B1084 to Wantisden. Ancient hollies and oaks. Snowdrops on the roadside verges; daffodils and bluebells in the woods around Butley.
Boyton Wood. To the right of the footpath as you pass the church and walk over the meadows to the River Tang is a remnant of ancient woodland. Badly damaged in the 1987 storm it has been replanted. Its boundary banks are probably medieval. Primroses, violets and bluebells abound in spring.

THE WALK

A well-signposted walk, quite easy going, with some stiles and Burrow Hill to climb. Thistles in summer, so take care if wearing shorts! Beautiful unspoilt isolated country by Butley river and the Ore. Good examples of marshland drained for arable and grazing land. Much of interest to bird watchers. Away from the rivers the walk traverses very pleasant farmland, meadows and woods.

TRANSPORT

Park: Butley Five Cross Ways. Map ref: 376495, Pathfinder 1031. Take the B1084 from Melton to Butley and turn right at pub.

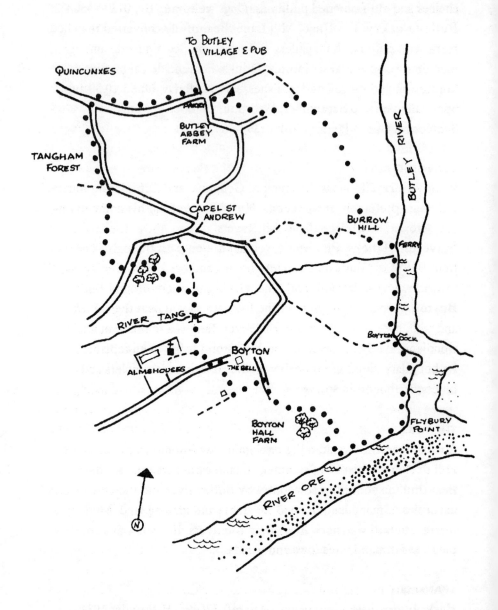

BUTLEY TO BOYTON

Five Cross Ways is about a mile down this road.

Buses: Regular service from Ipswich and Woodbridge.

7½ MILE WALK

With Butley village behind you, take the wide grassy track signposted to your left, going between fields. When you reach some rough ground with broom and pine, keep straight on until you come to a road. Turn left along it and in a short distance it becomes a sandy track leading to a T-junction where you turn right and follow the farm track across arable land and marsh. When you reach a stile and gate cross them and climb Burrow Hill. Go down the hill slightly to the right, cross the stile and turn left towards the river wall and ferry crossing. Turn right along the river wall which heads towards the sea. Where the Butley river meets the Ore the path turns right and you get a good view of Orford. Looking inland you can see cornfields edged with reeds marking the existence of a network of drainage channels and natural streams. The fields come almost up to the grassy river walls, some of which have lasted for around 700 years. Much of the area is now being flooded to re-instate the wet marshes. About half a mile from Flybury Point (where the wall turns right to run parallel with the Ore), you descend to the landward side of the wall and take the broad path ahead through the gate. Cross the fields towards some trees, where the path bears left with a drain on either side as well as a wood on the left. Continue straight ahead for about half a mile, then take a broad path to the left, between hedges. Just before you come to a house, turn right through the hedge and head across the field towards some houses in the far corner. Here the track enters a spinney to the right of a sign saying 'Private Property'. When you come onto the main road, turn right for the pub or left to continue the walk. A short distance along on the right is a sign to Boyton House; take this track as far as a fork where there is a big willow tree bearing a yellow waymark. The fork to the right leads you through a gate and along a path between stables on the right and trees on the left. The path meanders through a couple of meadows and crosses a wooden footbridge over the river Tang, into a field. (Its not easy to see the bridge as its hidden behind a mound, covered in nettles in summer.) About a third of the way up this field, the path cuts across it to the left towards the corner of Capel Wood. Follow the edge of this to the road where you cross onto the path opposite. At the end of this field, turn right and continue straight ahead to the lane. Keep straight ahead on this very quiet lane through attractive meadows and woods. Just past Green Farm you come to a T-junction; turn right and follow the pleasant wooded road back to Five Cross Ways, passing the daffodil and bluebell woods which are open to the public in the spring.

An alternative walk could be done, using the ferry to cross to Gedgrave, then walking into Orford. For a longer walk, from Orford, go through Sudbourne Park and Friars Walk to Chillesford and back to Butley (see Orford walk for details).

QUINCUNX
AT BUTLEY

BUTLEY TO BOYTON

TANGHAM FOREST

12

TANGHAM WAS THE FIRST site to be planted in Rendlesham forest in 1920 – 2,544 acres of, mainly, Corsican Pine. The deep, sandy soil here is formed from glacial sands and gravels. The underlying rocks are Red Crag and Chillesford clays and, in some places, Coralline Crag. Before the planting, the land was mainly heathland with some farmland and pasture containing very many small ponds which had a rich variety of plants both in and around them. The meadows were full of marsh marigolds, cowslips, ox-eye daisies, orchids, clovers, vetches and many more. The ponds in the peat-filled Tang valley today were specially created to replace these small, natural ponds. A meandering channel connects the ponds and aerates the water, allowing sticklebacks to thrive. They, in turn, attract kingfishers. A morsel of meadow survives to the right of the lane before you reach Green Farm in Capel St Andrew.

Most of Rendlesham Forest, including Tangham, was flattened in the 1987 gale, and 3,600 lorry loads of prime saw logs have been stored for future use; some 4,000 tonnes (200 lorry loads) were sold for commercial uses, such as building and paper-making. Instead of clearing all the debris, much of it was bulldozed into 'windrows'. You can see the result of this along the road from Woodbridge, around the Butley picnic site area. Walking among them, you will see that they are piled up at different angles and provide sheltered areas filled with different ages of new planting. By the time re-planting is complete, in 1996, over three million young trees, raised by the Forestry Commission, will have been planted out in this area. The debris in the windrows, is gradually breaking down, creating humus on which new plants are beginning to establish. Some of the windrows are covered in vegetation and already look very well established, others have barely begun to rot, and appear to be just a pile of tree roots, branches and trunks.

Clearing the timber exposed a number of interesting archaeological sites, mainly Anglo-Saxon burial mounds. These are protected, and will remain unplanted. Other clearings have deliberately been left in amongst the newly planted trees in order to provide light, which will encourage woodland flowers to grow. These, in turn, will attract butterflies, insects and seed-eating birds. Heathland clearings will encourage the breeding of woodlarks and nightjars, or fern owls as they are sometimes called. Another clearing has been used for an experiment. Pigs bred originally from woodland boars are being reared organically in the forest. As they root around, they clear the ground for future tree planting, just as their medieval ancestors might have done.

WHERE TO EAT
Butley Pottery and Tea Barn (see page 95).
The Oyster, Butley (see page 94).
The Froize, Chillesford (see page 94).

LOCAL INTEREST
The Phoenix Trail. The Forestry Commission leaflet, 50p from the machine, or from their office (if machine not working), provides a map of the Phoenix Trail with little snippets of information about the wildlife, etc. There are a number of waymarked paths to choose from to suit all ages and conditions of fitness. There are free toilets, including one for disabled people, at the car park.
Bike hire. Available from Easter to end September, daily 10am-4pm, at the car park. Charge £5 for half a day. They may close at midday if business is slack, so it may be wise to phone first if you want a bike in the afternoon. Pedal Power, Martlesham Heath. Tel: 01473- 610500.
Staverton Vineyard and Shop. Open Saturdays 10am-4pm. Signposted to the left (from Woodbridge direction) off B1084.

THE WALK
An easy walk on broad level, generally sandy or grassy tracks, through coniferous and deciduous woodland, bracken heath and farmland. Part

of the walk follows the Forestry Commission Phoenix Trail. There are shorter routes suitable for wheelchairs.

TRANSPORT

Park: at the right of the entrance to the Forest Enterprise site. Map ref: 354485, Pathfinder 1031. Turn off the B1084 at the sign for Tangham Camp site. Reach the car park after about one mile.
Buses: from Woodbridge to Orford, buses pass the entrance to Tangham Forest, about a mile from the start of the walk.

5 MILE WALK

From the car park, take the path past the information leaflet machine and follow the red-ringed posts. Cross straight over the tarmac track and, at a T-junction, turn right, cross the bridge over the pond and turn right again – the Tang valley is on your right. You may not see the river but you can see the willow, alder and birch scrub colonising the damp ground, with an isolated mature tree here and there. There are a number of small ponds along the valley. Water bubbling from springs in the crag is limy and suitable for frogs, toads and other amphibians. Paths lead down to the ponds where some picnic tables are provided. Keep following the red-ringed posts to a large storm-felled clearing to your right, with pines to your left. Here the red-marked path swings to the left; leave it and

KINGFISHER

TANGHAM FOREST

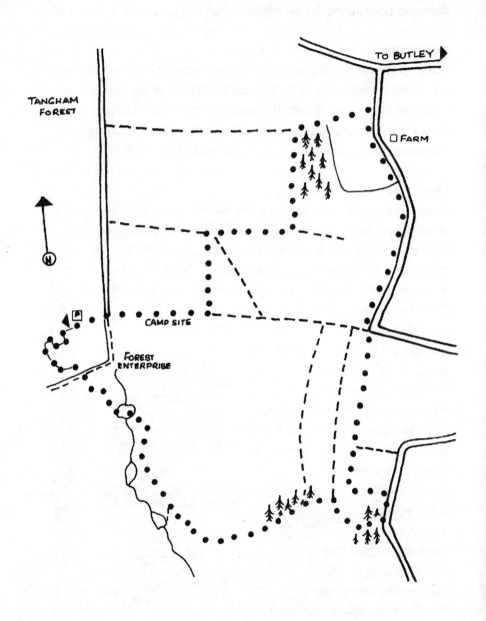

TANGHAM FOREST

continue straight on to the T-junction at the end of the pines. Turn right and head across the clearing to a stand of pines ahead. The path goes through this to a road where you turn left just as far as the large house, Ely Hill House. Turn left onto the bridleway at the side of the garden wall and follow it for some distance. The flattened forest is to the left and arable fields are to the right. When you come to a lane, carry on straight ahead along it. It is extremely quiet, and passes through very pretty woodland and meadows. Just after passing Green Farm on the right, turn left onto the cycle track through the forest. Shortly after passing the end of the field on your left, there is a broad track on the left (not waymarked); take this. You will come to a small clearing on the right and at the far side of it, turn right along a broad, sandy track. Shortly you come to a junction of several tracks. Ignore the first left, marked with a red and white striped post and the number four, but take the next left, a bridleway with a white waymark. This leads through young pine plantations. When you come to a track crossing, turn right. You go down past the campsite to the road, then straight ahead to the car park.

HONEY FUNGUS

TANGHAM FOREST

13

SUTTON TO SHOTTISHAM

SUTTON IS A LARGE PARISH stretching along the banks of the Deben from Shottisham Sluice, just north of Ramsholt nearly to Wilford Bridge at Melton. Most of the riverside land is privately owned, which has helped to keep its remote character unspoiled as it is inaccessible except on foot or by boat. It is criss-crossed by footpaths, a reminder of the times when sheep and shepherds wandered the heaths which must, at one time, have stretched to the saltings at the river's edge as evidenced by surviving names such as Sutton Walks, Heath Cottages and Bramble Hill. In the time of the Uffingas, it was an important part of the kingdom of East Anglia, and must also have been prosperous in the Middle Ages for it produced much wool which financed the building of a number of manor houses. Some still exist, including Wood Hall, originally built in 1566 on the site of the manor of Udsham, recorded in Domesday. Petistree Hall and Stokerland (now known as Ferry Farm) are two others. Methersgate, another medieval settlement with a landing place on the river, only got this name much later. The wool trade declined in the 18th century and the land became derelict, although it enjoyed a brief respite of affluence again during the Napoleonic wars when it was ploughed for corn which was then fetching high prices. In 1850, Stonner Quay was built for the coprolite barges. There were large quantities of coprolite in the area, and it was transported by barges from various quays along the Deben. The Hams and The Tips were built out into the river during the late 19th century by a farmer, Robert Knipe Cobbold, in an attempt to reclaim 150 acres of saltings. He'd intended they should reach further out into the river but Trinity House, afraid they'd alter the course of the river and interfere with shipping, put a stop to his plans.

There were several ferries crossing the river up until quite recently. Farmers often owned land on both sides of the river and had to cross

back and forth to tend it. Just north of Shottisham, you pass Sawpit
Covert. Coverts were originally planted for game girds in the 18th and
19th centuries. Two other commercial activities in the area were the
salt pans at Sutton and, since the 18th century, the area has been well
known for its carrots which thrive in the light sandy soil. Extensive use
of irrigation and plastic sheeting since 1979 has enabled farmers to
produce carrots and potatoes several weeks early.

WHERE TO EAT

The Plough, Sutton. Very pleasant low ceilinged, homely pub, very
much a local. Public bar with pool table, lounge bar and small dining
room. Grassy garden at back, overlooking open country. Small vine-
covered terrace to the side with pots of flowers. Typical dishes of
generous proportions are Suffolk ham, egg and chips, steak and kidney
pud and chicken piri piri. Three-course Sunday lunch £5.95. Children
welcome, dogs in public bar only. Tel: 01394-411785.
Sorrel Horse, Shottisham. A pretty thatched 14th-century smugglers'
inn. Serves sandwiches, burgers, jacket potatoes and Suffolk hotpot –
bacon, sausage and vegetables in a cheese sauce. Very reasonable
prices. Picnic tables on the green in front, newspapers in the bar. Dogs
and children under control welcome. Tel: 01394-411617.

LOCAL INTEREST

Sutton Hoo, Anglo-Saxon ship burial site. A group of low grassy mounds,
some of which have been excavated. Some of the treasures found are
to be seen in Woodbridge and Ipswich Museums. Most are in the
British Museum. It is thought to have been the grave of King Raedwald
who died in 624/5 AD. He is believed to have had a palace at
Rendlesham but nothing remains of it. Amongst the graves were found
what appeared to be a number of victims of execution or sacrifice.
Open April-September, Weekends 2-4pm £1.50. Contact A.A. Lovejoy,
Sutton Hoo Society, 28 Pembroke Road, Framlingham, IP13 9HA.

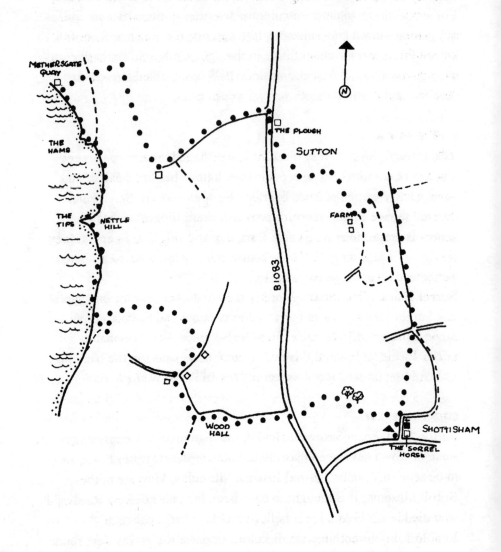

SUTTON TO SHOTTISHAM

A really beautiful walk along the northern bank of the river Deben, but check on the state of the tides before starting out as, due to erosion, parts of the foreshore are not passable when the tide is fully in. The inland part of the walk is through undulating fields, well endowed with trees, with gravel or sandy tracks or paved farm roads. Not a particularly easy walk in parts but well worth the effort. Wear stout shoes.

TRANSPORT

Park: in the pretty village of Shottisham, near the Sorrel Horse pub. Map ref: 320446, Pathfinder 1031.

Buses: regular service from Ipswich and Woodbridge to Bawdsey passes through both Sutton and Shottisham.

7 MILE WALK

With the pub and church to your right, walk down the dead end road until it bends to the right. Take the footpath straight ahead up the left side of Tower Cottage and turn left along the grassy path, to the right of the hedge. At the end of the field, go through the gap in the hedge and over the stile. Follow the path that bears slightly to the right, skirting the edge of the spinney. Cross a ditch via the footbridge, and continue straight ahead over the next field and another ditch, then bear left across to the far corner of the field onto the road. Cross the road and continue on the footpath which is up the drive leading to Wood Hall Hotel. The path skirts round to the right of the hotel, and continues straight ahead along an avenue of chestnuts to two small thatched flint cottages at the junction with a road. Take the right-hand fork. When you reach a large white brick house on the right (Sutton Hall), branch off to the left along a farm track. Ignoring the cross paths, keep on straight ahead passing two gates with stiles at the side. You are passing through fair-sized arable fields with small ridges of Scots pines. When you are nearly at the river, the path curves round to the left; leave it here, taking a path to the right, over a ditch into a field, through a hole in the hedge opposite and down to the river. After 100 yards or so, through reed beds, you come out onto a sandy beach. Keep along the beach till you reach the aptly named Nettle Hill – a high ridge of shelly sand covered in short grass and oak scrub, rising up from The Tips, a spit of land running out into the river. Walk round the spur of the hill, then immediately head inland into the trees, keeping to the right of the reeds. The path is not very clear here but it goes between some ash trees and winds up hill, then down again and up the other side where it flattens out slightly beneath the chestnuts. It's a few feet above the river and you'll have to clamber over the odd fallen tree. The path leads down to the shore again, near a spectacular fallen oak. You then come up onto the sea wall, with saltings to the left and a meadow to the right. Carry on round the bay, towards The Hams, the orangey cliffs ahead of you. The path here is very eroded, so walk along the top of the beach where you will see some striking arrangements of fallen dead trees and tangled roots protruding from the cliffs, only a matter of time before the soil is washed completely away from these trees and they too fall onto the beach. According to the map, a footpath goes inland from the top of the Hams but it is totally overgrown, so continue along the shore toward Methersgate Quay. The path goes through some trees, over a stile and alongside two arable fields. At the far side of the second, in front of a cottage, turn right and walk along the side of the field with the fence on your left. You will notice two parallel fences to your left with a ditch and vegetation between them. This is the official footpath! At the top of the field, there is a three-way footpath sign. Carry on straight ahead on a broad path through the crop. At a light-coloured gravel drive, turn right. To the left of this track is meadowland with a lot of willows and the grassy heath of News Hill rising up behind. Continue on this track, passing Cliff Farm and along an avenue of, mainly, sweet chestnuts to the main road where you turn right and cross over. The Plough is a short distance along on the left.

Immediately you pass the pub, take the footpath to the left and follow it round two sides of the field. You come to a broad sandy track. Turn right onto it. You pass a farm on the right then, opposite the first pair of semi-detached houses, take the track to the left. It's a pleasant sandy path between fields and trees. At the top of a rise, just past a cottage with its own water tower, take a track to the right. This is another very broad, sandy track and runs straight ahead for about ½ mile. When you come to a crossing of tracks, go straight over and, after a very few yards, fork right into the field and follow the path diagonally uphill to a stile. Cross this and walk down towards the village rooftops. Turn right at the bottom and follow the lane back to your car.

TREES ERODED BY THE RIVER DEBEN

SUTTON TO SHOTTISHAM

14 RAMSHOLT

RAMSHOLT IS A SAXON WORD meaning Ravenswood or Rams wood. It is mentioned in Domesday. The tower of the church is very old, possibly Roman and was built before the church, and used as a watch tower by the Saxons. It is built of local flint, septaria and brick but got covered by pink cement in a 1974 'restoration!'

It is thought that prior to the 15th century an arm of the river filled the depression below the church, to the north of the dock, and there may have been a quay and houses, but no records have been found to support this belief. This valley was flooded in the 1953 floods when the river wall was breached.

Until the 1880's, the land around was open fields and sheepwalks, then woods were planted to provide habitat for pheasants and other birds for shooting. At this time, about 200 people lived in the parish and, up until the beginning of this century, the dock was busy. There was a chicory maltings – chicory still grows in the hedgerows round here – and a lime kiln; the chicory and lime were exported in barges from the dock, along with coprolites and sugar beet. The barges brought in coal which was then distributed to the neighbouring villages. There were also fishing smacks and an oyster fishery, the remains of which can be seen in the mud along the river's edge north of Ramsholt. A ferry crossed the river to Kirton Creek until the 1920's. In the Middle Ages, ferries over the river here and elsewhere were very busy, linking a number of villages on both sides.

The present pub was known as the Ferry House in 1626 and as Dock Farm in 1838. The Dock Inn was at the top of the hill. There must have been severe weather here years ago as horses were unable to pull carts up the steep hill from the Dock if the weather was too bad, and had to take a road that ran from the pub through the dip between it and the church.

In the 1920's, there were 58 children attending the school; today it lies empty and only about 30 people currently live in Ramsholt. However, it's a very popular place with sailing folk and, in the summer, the river is full of all sorts of sailing boats.

An important feature of the area is the orangey Red Crag outcrop, a sandy mix of shells, fossils and iron compounds which has yielded up fossil teeth from sharks and woolly elephants, coral and seed pods, as well as bits and pieces of a variety of species of deer. There are specimens of this crag in the Ipswich museum showing very clearly the structure of this sort of rock. In the museum, you can also see several specimens of septarian nodules with their odd crystalline structure – not looking at all like the stuff that is used in building the church towers. It is composed of London clay mudstone through which water has seeped, depositing calcite (lime crystals). It occurs in layers about a foot thick, and was collected from shores and estuaries and dredged up from the sea bed. It is exposed on the surface in places along the Deben.

WHERE TO EAT

Ramsholt Arms. Beautiful situation with terrace overlooking the river and a garden. Interesting menu changes daily and includes fresh fish, local game and vegetarian dishes. Very tranquil, nothing here but the pub and jetty. But very popular boating place so gets busy in summer weekends and holidays. It was open all day in summer in 1994 and did cream teas, but it is now under new management, so that may change. Bed and breakfast also available, around £25 per person. Tel: 01394-411229.

If you want to picnic on the beach or paddle be sure to come when the tide is in, when there is a good stretch of sand in front of the pub.

THE WALK

An easy and idyllic walk in the right weather. Along the sandy shore of the Deben, across wet meadows and arable fields. The small and charming Ramsholt church is set in a delightfully overgrown

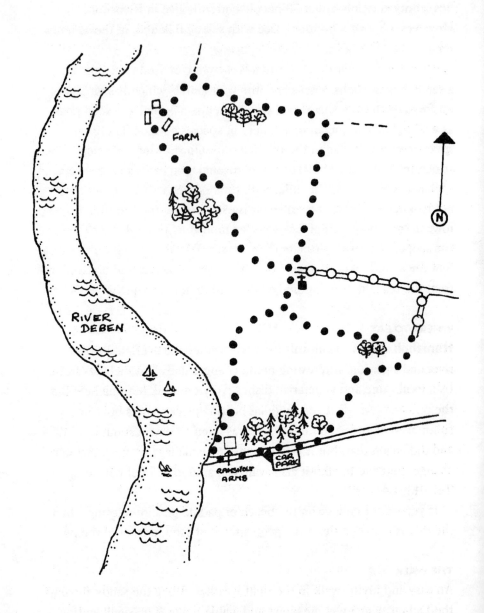

FARM

RIVER
DEBEN

N

RAMSHOLT
ARMS

CAR
PARK

RAMSHOLT

churchyard full of wild flowers such as valerian, scabious, thistles, mallow, cow parsley and others. There are stunning views down the river and you can get a good idea of how the area must have looked before the marsh and heath were reclaimed for agriculture. Further on are spectacular views up the Deben towards Waldringfield and Martlesham Creek. This walk is particularly good in July when wild flowers are abundant.

TRANSPORT

Park: in large car park at the top of the rise just before the entrance to the Ramsholt Inn, on the left-hand side. Map ref: 309414, Pathfinder 1031. Take B1083 to about half a mile past Shottisham, where you turn right, signposted to Ramsholt. After a further mile there is a sign to Ramsholt Inn, the turning after Ramsholt church.

3 MILE WALK

Leaving the car park, walk down towards the river on the surfaced path to the pub. At the shore, turn right and walk along the path clinging to the low sandy cliff. After a short distance, you veer right away from the river onto a broad grassy track meandering through wet meadowland and reed beds to the church. This shallow depression was once flooded by the river. The ground rises all around, clothed in a variety of trees. Just before you reach a junction of tracks, a small footpath goes up to the church. (The simple whitewashed church with its brick floor and box pews is worth a visit). Continue on the bridleway straight ahead up the side of a field and follow the orangey crag sand track around two sides of the very large field – there are Spanish chestnuts, pines, blue chicory, mallow, white campion, deadnettle and brambles in the hedgerows. The path then turns left towards Lodge Farm; follow it and continue on the still reddish sandy track all the way back to the church. Here you have a choice of routes; either continue straight ahead and turn right at the next footpath, or turn right down beside the church and turn left at the next signpost.

This path runs directly across the crop but it is clearly a path. At the far side of the field, the path comes out onto a broad bridleway – the one you'd be on if you had gone straight ahead at the church. Turn right and follow the bridleway as it bears round to the right, passing between a derelict school and a cottage. By a quintessential 'olde English' red-brick thatched cottage, complete with hollyhocks, the track divides. Follow the left-hand branch which leads down into a marshy dip full of meadowsweet, bullrushes, willows and wild hops, ragged robin, rosebay willow herb, and marsh thistle (in season!). The last stretch of this path is very shady, being quite densely overhung with trees. It brings you up to the road where you turn right and the car park is about 100 yards along on your left.

THE RAMSHOLT ARMS
FROM THE RIVER DEBEN

RAMSHOLT

THIS AREA WAS SETTLED in the late 5th century by the Scandinavians who established the Kingdom of East Anglia with its ruling dynasty, the Uffingas, who gave their name to Ufford. The Danes led by Uffa, sailed up the Deben and settled by a ford, so the story goes. It is thought that one of their kings, Raedwald, may have been buried at Sutton Hoo around 624AD, but only 'sand bodies' have been found there – detailed impressions in the sand of human bodies. These boat burials are unusual and are otherwise only found in Sweden around Uppland, so there must have been a link between Suffolk and Uppland at this time. It is believed that Raedwald had his palace at Rendlesham, just up the road, but no trace has ever been found of it.

Ufford's more recent claim to fame is as the birthplace of the Suffolk Punch horse, first foaled here in 1768. All of Suffolk's heavy horses since that date are descendants of that foal.

Early this century, Ufford held an annual ice carnival. At this time, the weather was such that the Deben, between Melton and Ufford, regularly flooded and froze over in winter. The trees were decorated and car headlights illuminated the dancers and ice hockey players.

The village of Bromeswell may have got its name from the large number of wells – some still in use – and the broom bushes which abound. Here also they grow willows for cricket bats and rushes for thatching. Bromeswell Common forms a nature reserve which starts behind the pub and stretches to the river bank and all the way to Wilford Bridge. It contains reed beds, grassland, woodland, and an orchid meadow. It is good nightingale country and there are numerous other birds, including the common and green sandpiper, greenshank, nine species of warbler, long-tailed tit, cuckoo, red poll, siskin, goldfinch, long-eared owl, and kingfisher.

THATCHED COTTAGES
AT UFFORD

Melton picnic site is also a nature reserve and notice boards there tell you what can be seen. There were once three quays here, at Wilford bridge, used by barges and schooners plying their trade on the Deben. At the beginning of the 19th century, there was talk of making the river navigable up to Debenham – an amazing prospect when you consider the river as it is around Ufford now.

WHERE TO EAT

The Lion, Lower Ufford. A pleasant, small and unpretentious old pub. Picnic tables on grass at the back overlook open countryside. Good, well-filled sandwiches. Bar snacks, including vegetarian. No dogs, children welcome in dining area (children's menu). Tel: 01394-460770.
The Cherry Tree, Bromeswell, Pleasant traditional beamed roadside inn with garden. Good selection of bar snacks around £3-£4, steaks and grills £6-10. Dogs allowed on leads. Tel: 01394-460310.
Wilford Bridge, Wilford Bridge Road, Melton. Traditional 'roadhouse' with good selection of bar snacks. Local fish a speciality. Take away service. Children's menu, no dogs (territorial pub dog on site!). Garden. Tel: 01394-386141.

LOCAL INTEREST

Bromeswell Green and Wilford Bridge Wildlife Site (SWT).

Entrance from Common Lane. Woodland, grassland and reedbed on bank of the Deben. 300+ plant species including southern marsh orchid.

Ufford Church. Small Norman church. The 15th-century, 18-foot-tall, elaborately carved font cover is world renowned. It still retains some of its colouring and is topped by a carved pelican. Many of the original 15th-century benches remain and are of traditional East Anglian design with richly ornamental ends carved from oak planks.

Drift Nursery. A short distance along from The Cherry Tree; an unusual and interesting nursery selling mainly alpines.

Sutton Hoo. (see page 105).

THE WALK

A fairly easy walk at first, but around Bromeswell, the footpaths have not been well kept, and care has to be taken in the meadow off School Lane. The path through the reed beds from Bromeswell Common Lane back to Wilford Bridge may not be passable at high tide. But don't be put off; just wear waterproof footwear and take a stick. Cormorants fish near Wilford Bridge, herons along the river.

TRANSPORT

Park: Melton riverside car park, just before Wilford Bridge on the right side of the A1152 from Woodbridge. Map ref: 296504, Pathfinder 1008.

Buses: regular services pass the car park.

Trains: Melton station is close by (on the Ipswich-Lowestoft line).

4½ MILE WALK

Take the footpath from the far (E) end of the car park, and follow the path marked by a white arrow, lined with brambles, wild roses and hawthorn, to the right. When you get to the river wall, turn left along it. At the bridge, cross the road and fork left along Wilford Bridge Lane. After passing an old water-filled quarry on the right, the lane

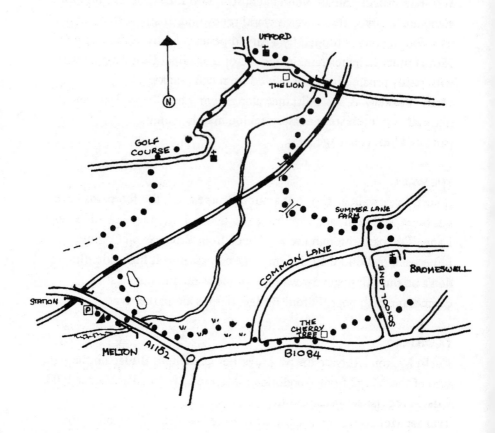

MELTON TO UFFORD

crosses the railway line and continues straight ahead. Just past a large
brick garage, the track bears left. Leave it here, taking the sandy path
up to the right and follow it round the right-hand side of the field.
At the T-junction, keep straight on towards a house. This brings you
to a road with a golf course opposite. Turn right along the road a short
distance to a footpath sign on the left. Climbing the rather steep stile,
take this path which runs diagonally over the golf course, or walk
around the edge. Cross the second steep stile and turn left onto the
quiet road to Lower Ufford. You arrive in the village opposite the post
office. Turn left and then right into the lane leading to the church.
You pass some very attractive cottages with beautiful gardens and the
18th-century stocks and whipping post at the church gates. Follow the
footpath through the churchyard round to the right of the church,
through another gate and out opposite The Lion. Turn left along the
road here, cross the bridge over the River Deben and turn
immediately right. The grassy path follows the river for a while, then
shortly after crossing a stile, turn left, away from the river and along
the edge of the meadow. This path is neither marked nor obvious, but
there is a stream to its left and you follow this until you come to a
bridge over it. Cross this and the railway line. The footpath goes
diagonally across the corner of the field in front but the footpath sign
has been uprooted. At the far side, you will come to another footpath
sign at a bridge over the ditch. Cross this and turn left around the next
field. Shortly before the end of the field, the path veers left towards
the farmhouse. It is quite overgrown for some yards and a stick to
flatten the nettles would be an asset. The path skirts the farmhouse
garden and emerges onto a sandy track by the gate to Summer Lane
Farm. Continue ahead to the road where you turn left. When the road
bends to the left, take the footpath to the right. It traverses a field,
passes the backs of some gardens, crosses a lane and continues slightly
to the right. This is a broad, shady path, passing through a patch of
heathland. After a short distance, you follow the waymarked path
downhill to the right, emerging on School Lane, Bromeswell. Turn left

for about 100 yards and you will find a footpath to the right. It is not a well-trodden path, just a broad swathe cut through grass, and could be a little hazardous as the surface is uneven. There are two ditches without any means of getting across, apart from jumping – not too difficult if you are reasonably agile. The path continues between the old fish ponds and emerges at the Cherry Tree pub. Here it is necessary to walk along the road for about 150 yards but there is a grass verge. Turn right into Common Lane and after about 50 yards there is a footpath sign to the left, rather hidden in the trees. As long as it is not high tide you can take this path which runs through the reed beds and comes out on the road near Wilford Bridge. From the bridge cross the road and take the footpath back to the car park.

SUFFOLK PUNCH HORSES
AT WORK

MELTON TO UFFORD

THE MEDIEVAL PORT OF GOSEFORD – a ford haunted by
geese – stretched down the Deben from about Kirton Creek to
Felixstowe, or Fileth Stowe, meaning either a place of felled trees or a
place of hay. The latter is thought to be more likely as the seashore
was covered by Marram grass; the trees started further inland. Guston, of
which no trace remains, was a small customs port in a bay somewhere
around what is now Kirton and Falkenham Creeks.

Goseford was a wide expanse of water with marshy inlets, channels
and landing places. The Kings Fleet, a branch of the Deben, formed
the main anchorage, sheltered as it was by the higher ground of Walton.
Ideas about the derivation of its name differ. It is said that Edward III
marshalled his fleet there before going off to fight the French. Some
say the name is connected with Charles I who inaugurated
drainage schemes with Dutch engineers, 'fleet' being from
the Old English for creek or inlet. Whatever its
origins it is now a shadow of its former self. Land
reclamation for farming started long ago and
has left the Kings Fleet as just a sluice
controlled backwater.

Before the sea walls were built, there were
islands of crag and gravel in the Kings Fleet marshes,
settled by the Anglo-Saxons. Names ending in -ey and
-ay signify these island sites.

In the Middle Ages, Goseford haven became a
busy port for the wool trade, exporting Suffolk
cloth, to the low countries, and an important
fishing port. When Edward III and his court
stayed at Walton Castle, they ate an enormous
amount of fish and the religious houses in the area

SEA
LAVENDER

were great consumers of local fish. So both sea and in-shore fishing became the main local industry. Fishing weirs, wattle fences which formed a 'V' with a basket to hold the fish at the pointed end, covered the sandbanks.

Felixstowe was once much further out to sea. A wide stretch of common land called Middleton common had, by the 18th century, been worn away except for a band of septaria forming Cobbold's point. Man helped in the erosion of the cliffs of Felixstowe, digging out septaria for building stone. It was used in 1500 to build the tower of St. Mary's church in Trimley, and Cardinal Wolsey managed to get some to start building his college in Ipswich.

About quarter of a mile out to sea, off The Dip, lie the ruins of Walton Castle. Recent diving explorations have confirmed it to be of Roman origin, built as part of a chain of forts to defend the coast against the Saxon invaders. Earlier this century, the ruins could still be seen at very low spring tides.

The sea walls at the mouth of the Deben were started very early on. There are records of grants being made to tenants at Walton to build walls and enclose land in 1321, and of an agreement with marshland tenants to repair some walls around the Kings Fleet before 1500.

In the late 15th century, new shipbuilding methods produced larger ships and Woodbridge, with its shipbuilding activities and its agricultural hinterland producing goods for transport from the area, became more important than Goseford, so Goseford declined. The ever-shifting Deben bar at the mouth of the river has always presented difficulty to shipping and dictated the size of ship that could use the river thus preventing – or saving – the Deben from becoming the sort of commercial river that the Orwell became.

At Felixstowe Ferry, there are records of a Ferry House on the site of the Ferry Boat Inn since 1181. The present inn, built on a shingle bank, has a frame of huge oak beams which have held it stable on the shingle for years. In the 15th century, there was a fish market here, and still the local fishermen sell their catch from huts on the beach.

In the 19th century, bricks were made in the Kirton area and taken by barge from Kirton Dock. Inland from Kirton Creek, Corporation Farm (which you pass on one of the walks) was built on land willed by William Smart in 1598 to the 'bailiffs, burgesses and commonality of Ipswich' for charitable use. The revenues were used for the maintenance of the children of poor Freeman at the Ipswich Free School.

Over the river from Felixstowe Ferry is Bawdsey Manor, where Radar was developed in the 1930s, when it belonged to the Air Ministry. The chain ferry started at the end of the 19th century and has always been in the hands of the Brinklely family. Now a motor boat, the ferry is under threat because land has changed hands. Bawdsey Manor has become a school.

WHERE TO EAT

The Fox, Newbourne. Near to, but not on, route of Hemley walk. For details see page 00.

The Victoria, Felixstowe Ferry. Attractive bar, lots of wood and an unusual mural of smugglers smuggling. Garden at side and a few tables in front. Varied menu includes vegetarian dishes, baguettes and 'doorsteps'. Dogs welcome outside mealtimes. Tel: 01394-271636.

The Ferry Boat, Felixstowe Ferry. Recent refurbishment has retained some of the original feel of an old-time cross Channel ferry boat. Picnic tables under front verandah and on grass. Varied menu. Well-behaved dogs welcome. Tel: 01394-284203.

Ferry Café. Open daily all year from 8am (7am at weekends) until 5pm, last orders 4.30pm. All-day 'Ferry breakfast' is everything you can think of in a fried breakfast plus toast, marmalade and tea. Sandwiches to take away. Tel: 01394-276305.

LOCAL INTEREST

Newbourne Springs Nature Reserve (see page 139).
Landguard Nature Reserve and Bird Observatory (SWT) at the

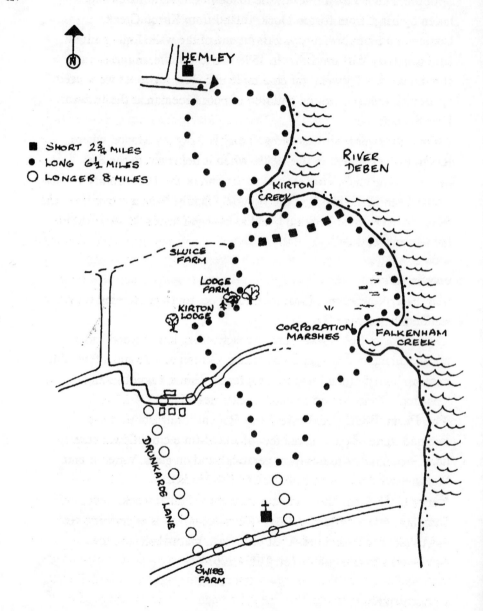

HEMLEY

RIVER DEBEN

■ SHORT 2¾ MILES
● LONG 6½ MILES
○ LONGER 8 MILES

KIRTON CREEK

SLUICE FARM

LODGE FARM

KIRTON LODGE

CORPORATION MARSHES

FALKENHAM CREEK

DRUNKARDS LANE

SWIBS FARM

AROUND THE RIVER DEBEN

opposite end of Felixstowe on the Orwell Estuary. This SSSI is well worth a visit. There are 16 hectares of compacted shingle and scrub seashore with outstanding spring and summer flora, including rare suffocated and clustered clovers. It is one of only three places in Britain where stinking goosefoot grows. There are also 23 recorded species of butterfly as well as a number of rarities from the bird world. GR 285315. Park at entrance to reserve. Sea front summer Sunday bus. **Public toilets** opposite Ferry Café.

Fresh fish sold from sheds past Ferry Café.

HEMLEY, KIRTON CREEK AND FALKENHAM CREEK WALKS

All these walks have stunning views along the river Deben. Inland is pleasant undulating farmland, with small woods and spinneys. The few short road stretches are very quiet. There are birds, flowers and butterflies in abundance, depending on the seasons. Boots or strong shoes are advisable and it's also not a good idea to have bare legs when walking through reeds!

TRANSPORT

Park: on the road near Hemley church. Map ref: 286423, Pathfinder 1031.

WALK 1 2³/₄ MILES

From Hemley church, walk down towards the river, following the footpath sign straight ahead on a broad, sandy track that passes some pretty wooden cottages. Where this path bends to the right, take the path slightly to the left between tall grassy hedges, towards the river. As you pass an overgrown pond with reed beds, there is another sign directing you slightly to the right towards the river wall. As you come out onto the marshes, turn right along the well-worn, sandy path on the river wall along the edge of the marshes. To its right is a parallel track at the edge of the marsh that could be boggy in wet weather. Care needs to be taken where a stream from the river crosses the path and you need to leap a small ditch. Just before you reach Kirton Creek,

AROUND THE RIVER DEBEN

there is a group of dead trees on the right and the path rises, passing through a tunnel of blackthorn. The raised path continues with the creek on your left, reed beds and a stand of poplars on your right. When you reach the head of the creek, descend onto the broad track and turn left round the creek. Cross the creek wall and continue with the wall on your left. When you come to a small inlet from the river, take a path inland up the right-hand side of a field, with a clump of bushes on the right. This will bring you to the lane running more or less parallel with the southern side of Kirton Creek. You come to the path leading down to the creek on the right – the same path you take coming from the other direction on the longer walks. Turn right here, downhill, past the head of the creek, then uphill back to Hemley church. This path is quite rutted from farm vehicles but it is wide, and in June, is awash with butterflies.

WALK 2 6½ MILES

Proceed from Hemley church as in the first walk as far as the 'small inlet from the river'. This time, continue along the path – in the lea of the wall if it's a cold and windy day or climb onto the wall for fabulous views of the river as you walk along. Follow either of these paths nearly all the way around Falkenham Creek, a wide expanse of marsh and shallow lagoons full of wading birds. When you come to a footpath sign pointing right, inland, follow this across the field. You come to a patch of tarmac and two sandy paths; take the one to the left, a nice wide easy track between high banks of

SUFFOCATED CLOVER

vegetation. At a sign pointing right, follow this path as it rises up from the valley bottom. You are now at a junction with a signpost pointing along the lane to the left. Ignore this and continue straight ahead, following the yellow waymark, which is not obvious. Almost immediately, the path turns round to the right in front of a large piece of concrete hardstanding. It continues as a broad, sandy path, with hedges on either side. On the right, you pass a spinney then go downhill and up the next rise. When you come to a sort of T-junction where the path to the left leads to some farm buildings and cottages (Corporation Farm), take the right fork and very shortly, at another signpost, turn left over the field. The footpath across the crop is quite clear. At the far side of the field, turn right and follow the edge of the field, with trees on your left. At the hedge at the end, turn left towards a rusty gate and follow the path to the right of the low chainlink fence. The attractive grounds of Kirton Lodge are on your left. The easy grassy path reaches a confluence of tracks; keep straight on between hedges of wild rose, hawthorn and brambles. Carry on until you reach a T-junction, where you turn right. You will see Kirton Creek ahead to your left, and a footpath about 200 yards along on the left will lead you down to it. Continue on past the head of the creek. Veering slightly left the path leads back up to Hemley church.

WALK 3 8 MILES

Proceed as for the second walk around Falkenham Creek, along the sandy path and the next path that 'rises up from the valley bottom'. At this junction, follow the sign to the left, passing a small wood on your right. When you reach an iron gate in the hedge leading into the churchyard, go through this, through the churchyard and out another iron gate onto the road, where you turn right. Continue along this road through the village until you come to Swiss Farm. Almost opposite, you will find a bridleway going across the field to the right – this is Drunkards Lane. Follow this and continue on it when it becomes a

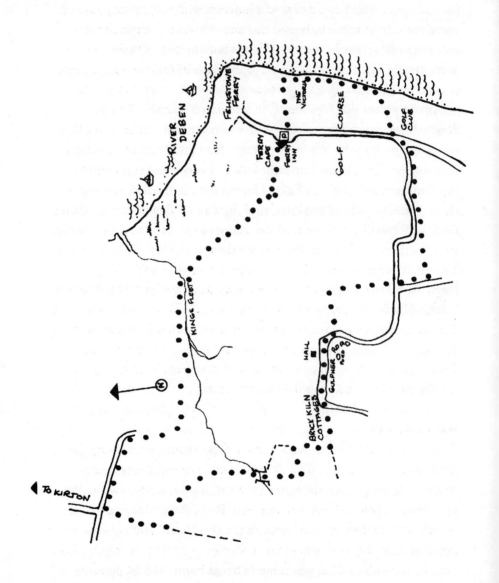

AROUND THE RIVER DEBEN

paved lane, going uphill to Corporation Farm. Past the farm barns, the lane does a sharp left bend. Here you go right, keeping the barns on the right and, near some cottages on the left, you will see a signpost in the hedge with 'Private road, keep to footpath'. Follow the cinder track round to the left where you come to the 'sort of T-junction' described in Walk 1. Follow directions for Walk 1 back to Hemley church.

FELIXSTOWE FERRY

This walk takes you across wide open country over arable farmland and down to the shore, showing you the width and shallowness of the river valley with its almost imperceptible rise to the Trimleys to the south and the higher cliffs of Bawdsey on the north bank. You also see the sea breaking over the constantly shifting shingle bars at the mouth of the estuary.

TRANSPORT

Park: in car park alongside the road in front of the Ferry Inn. Map ref: 328377, Pathfinder 1054.
Bus: regular service, and Felixstowe sea front summer Sunday service.

7 MILE WALK

Turn left onto the road towards the river. Just before the Ferry Café, turn left between some railings onto an asphalted footpath. On the right, you pass a clutter of sheds, houseboats, sailing boats, old hulks, beach houses with little gardens and, beyond that, the Deben estuary. On your left is the tail end of the golf course. At some posts with a yellow waymark, turn right and continue along the top of the river wall. Shortly after the path goes round a stile, it curves inland around the head of an inlet and you find a footpath sign pointing inland. Descend from the wall and follow the broad track straight ahead through some gates. This track runs through reclaimed marshland, alongside the Kings Fleet, for about ¾ mile. There is a wind pump on the bank of the Kings Fleet and to the right, you can see the river wall curving along the Deben into the distance. As you leave the former marshes, the landscape changes. The fields now have hedges and oak trees. Just after the start of the hedge, the road curves round to the right and rises up through cornfields to Deben Lodge Farm. When you come to a bar across the road and a step-over fence, carry straight ahead past the farm. As the road bends to Kirton, you will find the footpath signed over the fields to the left. It cuts through the crop but is well walked and clearly marked. When you come down into a dip, the ground is rather damp and covered in young willow and alder trees. Turn left into the trees along the valley bottom – don't be put off by its overgrown look. After a few yards, the undergrowth disappears and the path emerges by a small lake with a nesting box for water fowl. Walk along the right-hand side of this to a stile, the path is waymarked over it. Just ahead is another stile with two waymarks. Don't follow the left-hand one, it doesn't get you anywhere. Follow the one that points slightly right, towards the end of a hedge and fence posts going partway up the meadow on the right. When you get to the end of the hedge, turn right and follow along the fence to the corner. Here you climb over a piece of three-barred fence and cross the wooden footbridge over the very end of the Kings Fleet. From here, the footpath heads diagonally across the field to some trees. As there is no sign of this on the ground, follow round the right-hand edge of the field and left at the top until you get to a farm track. Turn right towards a red house (Brick Kiln Cottages). Passing this, the track bends left onto Hill House Track and joins a paved road (Gulpher Road). Go straight down the road, past Gulpher Duck Pond on the right and Gulpher Hall on the left then, as the road does a bit of an S-bend, just past a house with an orange pantiled mansard roof, turn left onto a grassy footpath. Slightly raised between two fields, it offers lovely views over to the river and is very colourful in autumn. Follow the path round the edge of the field, ignoring the exit over a stile to your left, and carry straight ahead until you come to a road junction. Take the road straight ahead and just where the houses begin is a footpath to the left. Follow this; it emerges on the road (Ferry Road) at a sharp bend by a World War II pill box. Turn right onto the road and continue along it until you come out opposite the golf club. Turn left onto the road, walk a short distance and, just after a row of trees on the right is a footpath sign pointing over the golf course. Take this and walk past the next waymarked post, up onto the sea wall. Turn left along the broad, asphalted promenade at the back of the beach. Follow this past the two martello towers and a row of houses. Here you come to some steps leading down to The Victoria pub. From there, you can carry on to the next set of steps that bring you down opposite where you parked the car.

FELIXSTOWE FERRY

AROUND THE RIVER DEBEN

17 TRIMLEY TO LEVINGTON

T HE AREA AROUND Trimley was once extensively settled, both
by Anglo-Saxons and Romans. Just inland from Levington, at
Nacton Heath, is a group of tumuli, known as the Seven Hills – the site
of an old Danish settlement and probably a battle between the Danes
and the Romans. Aerial photographs show quite extensive field
markings. Many of the names you'll see around, such as Grimston,
Alston and Morston, appear in Domesday. In Norman times, there
were salt pans on the marshes below Grimston Hall. Salt was
evaporated from sea water in shallow depressions in which the water
level was controlled by sluices. It is not known when the river walls
here were built but they probably put paid to the salt industry by
cutting off the supply of sea water.

Large quantities of shrimps and mussels from the beds in Levington
Creek were sold in Ipswich fish market from the 13th century and
there were many fish weirs along the foreshore. In the 14th century,
the Port of Ipswich was given jurisdiction over maritime matters along
the whole length of the Orwell. Peripatetic 'Admiralty Courts' were
held on the hards all along the river, including the one at Levington
Creek. They adjudicated on all maritime disputes, proclaimed fishing
seasons and the size of nets. In the early 1600's a large ferry ran from
Harwich to Ipswich, charging one penny for a trip to market on Saturdays.

In the time of Henry VIII, the whole area from Brightwell to Walton
and down to the river was a great stretch of heathland, called Cawdwell
Heath. It remained mostly unenclosed until the 19th century, when
the sandy tracks were turned into paved roads.

Coprolite was first used in Levington in 1717, more than 100 years
before the industry took off. Later, when coprolites were being
exploited commercially, people in Levington were digging up their
gardens to sell the coprolite found there, getting as much as £20 for a

evidence of the return of the rabbits around this area and, presumably, the wire net fences around the fields are rabbit-proofing. The track climbs up the other side of the valley to the Brightwell Road. Cross straight over to the path on the far side. You soon come to cross tracks; take the broad, sandy farm track opposite, downhill and round to the right. As the path starts to rise, just before some buildings, is a gate with an old notice 'Beware of the Bull' and a footpath sign to the left. There will probably be no bull (there are certainly no signs of any cattle having been in this field), so follow the waymarks and you will come to a concrete bridge across the river. Bear right across the field towards the cottages and a gate onto the main road, where again you cross directly onto the footpath on the far side. This broad, sandy track leads through some farm buildings and curves left just in front of the last buildings. Follow this path until, a short distance before the road, you find a footpath, not signposted, across the field to your left. It's not easy to see but it runs just to the right of a small oak tree, then directly across to the far side of the field, coming out by the lay-by where you started.

THE FOX INN
AT NEWBOURNE

BRIGHTWELL TO NEWBOURNE

BIBLIOGRAPHY

Arnott, WG, Alde Estuary, Norman Allard 1952
Arnott, WG, Orwell Estuary, Norman Allard 1954
Arnott, WG, Suffolk Estuary, Norman Allard 1950
Armstrong, Patrick, The Changing Landscape, Terence Dalton 1975
Bacon, J&S, Aldeburgh Suffolk, Segment Publications 1984
Bacon, J&S, The Suffolk Shoreline and the Sea, Segment Publications 1984
Beardell CH, Dryden RC& Holzer TJ, The Suffolk Estuaries,
    Suffolk Wildlife Trust report, Segment 1991
Chadwick, Lee, In Search of Heathland, Dennis Dobson 1982
Countryside Commission, Suffolk Coast and Heath Landscape,
Edlin, HL (Ed), East Anglian Forests, HMSO 1972
Edwards, Russell, The Suffolk Coast, Terence Dalton 1991
Fitter, R&A & Blamey, M, The Wildflowers of Britain and Northern Europe,
    Collins 1985
Jennings, Celia (Ed), Suffolk For Ever, Alastair Press 1989
Kinsey, Gordon, Orford Ness, Secret Site, Terence Dalton 1981
Maycock, Colin, Charity, Clay & Coprolites, Mary Warners Charity 1993
Moore, Derek (Ed), Watching Wildlife in Suffolk,
    Suffolk Wildlife Trust Reserve Guide 1994
Morgan, Geoffrey, East Anglia, Its Tideways and Byways, Robert Hale 1991
Open University, Ecology Course S326, Open University Press 1985
Pennington, Winifred, The History of British Vegetation,
    English University Press 1974
Sanford, Martin, Orchids of Suffolk, Suffolk Naturalists Society 1991
Scarfe, Norman, The Suffolk Landscape, Alastair Press 1972 (revised 1987)
Scarfe, Norman, The Suffolk Guide, Alastair Press 1960 (revised 1988)
Simper, Robert, The Suffolk Sandlings, East Anglian Magazone Publishing 1986
Simpson, Francis, Simpson's Flora of Suffolk, Suffolk Naturalists Society 1982
Suffolk Wildlife Trust, Sandlings Annual Report, 1993/4
Suffolk Women's Institute, Suffolk Village Book, Suffolk Federation of
    Women's Institutes 1991
Trist, PJO, Agricultural Survey of Suffolk, Royal Agricultural Society 1971
Whitehead, RA, The Beloved Coast, Terence Dalton 1991
Parish booklets produced by various churches

A fairly easy walk with beautiful views, along the Orwell with its shipping and wooded valley sides rising from saltmarsh or mudflats.

TRANSPORT

Park: At the end of Thorpe Lane by the Goslings Track notice. Leave the A14 to Trimley villages. At the roundabout turn right. Turn into Grimston Lane, about ½ mile along on your left and continue straight ahead over the level crossing. Map ref: 265377, Pathfinder 1056.
Buses: regular services from Ipswich and Felixstowe to Trimley.

5½ MILE WALK

Take the bridleway signposted to the left and at the next sign, turn right across the stile and follow the footpath downhill, under the trees (muddy in wet weather). It bends to the left and, at the bottom of the hill, comes to a T-junction. Turn right and the path rises uphill again, where you come out onto a broad, sandy track by some cottages. Follow the path to just before the level crossing where you turn left onto Morston Hall track. Follow the yellow waymarks on the stile and gates through the farm, and continue straight ahead, with a tall hedge on your right. The path leads through a hedge and down a bracken-covered slope then up alongside another, vast, field. At the road, turn left to the marina, then turn right, keeping to the outer – landward – side. Continue to the far end, where you go up onto the new bank between silt pans – could be very muddy in wet weather. Carry on around Levington Creek to some rails; turn right through a blackthorn thicket and follow the grassy path up the field towards the church. You come out opposite The Ship. On the return, turn left out of the pub and walk down the road. Turn right onto a concrete track to the head of the creek and up onto the footpath leading back to the marina. Continue right through the marina and, just past the old red light ship, now the yacht club, take the path up the sandy cliff. This runs beneath trees, eventually coming onto a causeway between the river

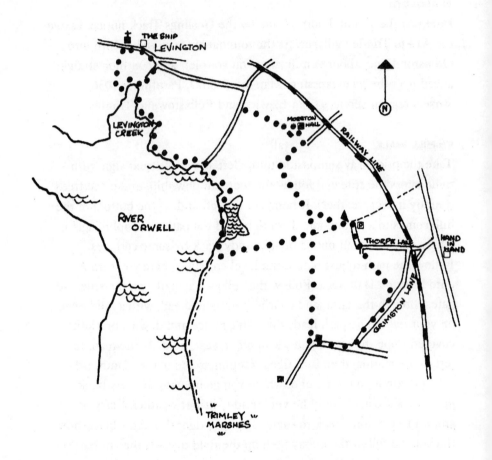

TRIMLEY TO LEVINGTON

and the fishing lake. At the end of the causeway is a beach. Take the sandy footpath to the left, leading uphill away from the river. When you reach a gate at the end of a shrubbery, turn right and follow the bridleway, which leads down to a white cottage with an orange mansard roof and pretty garden. Turn left here and follow the lane, Grimston Lane, round the next left-hand bend, and straight ahead until you come to a footpath by two oak trees, leading over the field to your left. Follow this, past Goslings Farm to where you left your car.

To extend the walk round the nature reserve, don't turn inland when you reach the beach at the end of the causeway; continue straight ahead and the path takes you round the perimeter of the nature reserve, on the river wall. At a junction, turn left up to Searsons Farm, where again you turn left and head for Grimston Hall. Turn left here, past Alston Hall. When you come to the junction with Grimston Lane, turn right and follow it to the footpath that takes you over the field and back to the car. This will add about 4½ miles to the walk.

GRIMSTON LANE
TRIMLEY

TRIMLEY TO LEVINGTON

BRIGHTWELL TO NEWBOURNE

AROUND 22, largely Bronze Age, barrows existed on Brightwell and Martlesham Heaths and they were partly excavated in 1953 just before the heath was ploughed up. The barrows hadn't remained undisturbed until modern farming flattened them though, they had been disturbed throughout the centuries by treasure hunters, tree planters and rabbits – to select just a few causes. Besides evidence of Bronze Age cremation, there were bits of pottery from both the early Iron Age and the pre-Bronze Age. Heathland stretched most of the way from Ipswich to Waldringfield at the beginning of this century, and 2,500 sheep grazed around Brightwell and Newbourne.

Behind the village hall there are the remains of a hill of sand. Many tons of it were dug from here to build Felixstowe Docks in the 1960s. The few houses of Brightwell are in the valley of the Mill River – a mere stream now – that winds its way to Kirton Creek and the Deben. In the days of Guston, it was deeper and formed a wide estuary where the inhabitants of Newbourne had fishing weirs at Kirton Creek. Until the present road was built through Brightwell in the 1920's, the river formed a ford over the road. Brightwell means a clear spring or well and there are several springs in the valley.

Newbourne lies in a sheltered, sunny valley in attractive, undulating country. About 100 years ago, it was just a church, a pub, a hall and a few cottages. Then in 1934, the Land Settlement Association, set up to deal with the problem of unemployment in the depression, bought 200 acres around Newbourne and built 50 houses on it. They imported unemployed Durham miners, trained them in horticulture and allocated them each to a small holding where they could grow outdoors or under glass, and keep pigs and poultry. Twenty years later, the Settlement was self-supporting, but in 1983 the Ministry of Agriculture abolished it. Ten of the local growers formed a co-operative and produced salad crops for the co-op, Newbourne Growers Ltd. This has now grown to a large co-op of around a hundred growers, stretching to Essex, Cambridgeshire and Lincolnshire. You cannot miss seeing the acres of glasshouses around Newbourne.

Newbourne Springs used to supply water to the Felixstowe area, pumping half a million gallons a day for the Felixstowe Water Company. However, nitrate levels were found to be too high and the pumping had to stop. The springs, now a nature reserve, belong to Anglian Water and is managed for them by the Suffolk Wildlife Trust.

WHERE TO EAT

The Fox, Newbourne. It is said that in the 13th century, a river flowed near the site of this inn and there was an upturned boat beside it, used as a dwelling. Some time later, a permanent building was constructed using the timbers of the original boat. Since 1634, this building has been a traditional inn, not much altered over the years. Picnic tables in front and in the garden at the side. Outdoor skittles. An imaginative menu, reasonable prices, several vegetarian choices and a children's menu. Freshly prepared, home-grown or local produce. Morning coffee from 10.30 am. Cream teas in the summer. Tel: 01394-736307.

LOCAL INTEREST

Newbourne Springs Nature Reserve. Open at all times. Information centre at the old Pump House by the pub. There is a waymarked path round the reserve, which is rich in plantlife, birds, animals and insects. The many springs make their way down the valley sides to a fast-flowing stream where a variety of water plants grow. Alder carr has developed and fen and reed beds on abandoned cattle marshes. On drier ground, spotted and twayblade orchids flourish and violets, primroses and bluebells in spring. Tree creepers, spotted flycatchers, kingfishers, herons, green sandpipers, warblers, redwings, blackcaps can all be found and the, now scarce, song thrush nests here. A number of small mammals, reptiles and amphibians also live in the reserve. On the wall of the information centre is a list of all the birds seen in the area. Car park at Information centre. Opposite the car park is a disused coprolite pit and sand martins often nest in the crag. In the fossil layer at the base of the crag have been found bones and teeth from whales and dolphins and other fish.

Brightwell Church originally dates from 1300, built of local rubble. It has been much restored and renovated over the centuries. The entry arch is original and the door is medieval.

THE WALK

A fairly easy walk, if a little hilly for Suffolk, on mainly sandy or grassy tracks through farmland, and the attractive swampy, woodland of Newbourne Springs and the Mill River valley.

TRANSPORT

Park: in small lay-by on the Waldringfield Road, at the junction with Newbourne Road. Map ref: 255439, Pathfinder 1031.
Bus: regular service from Ipswich and Woodbridge to Waldringfield.

5½ MILE WALK

Turn right onto the Waldringfield road and walk to the bend at Sheep Drift Cottages. Take the bridleway, signposted, on the far side of the road, following it downhill, parallel with the road. At the signpost, turn right over the stile and cross the main road where the track continues through trees – sweet chestnut, oak, brambles and other vegetation make a pleasant shady path. Heathland with birch scrub and bracken rises sharply to your left. After a good half mile, you pass a small pond/reservoir and the ground starts sloping uphill. To the left, a path goes down into the scrub between two wire fences. To its left is marsh and bracken, with the land rising up behind it. Follow this path through the trees along the edge of a field and over a stile, along the next field (full of ragwort) at the end of which you turn right up the slope. Near the top of this field, a footpath sign directs you to the left and over a stile. The footpath goes between some trees but can be a bit overgrown in patches. You can walk along the edge of the field just to the left. You come onto a broad track with marshy ground to the left, bullrushes, rosebay willow herb and willow scrub. The soil here is very sandy and orangey. Some little distance along on the left is a stile crossing into Newbourne Springs Nature Reserve – worth a visit. It has a variety of habitats, heath on the tops of the slopes, swamp, alder carr, dry woodland, tall fen and reed bed. The path becomes a lane with some well-manicured gardens and houses, and brings you down to The Fox public house. From the pub, turn right up the road and, at the first junction, right again into Ipswich Road, past the church and up the rise. At the end of the council houses on your left is the footpath. As it bends to the left, you will find another path to the right with a stile into a field where, if you are faced with an electric fence, follow round the edge and exit by a stile at the top. Turn right onto a broad path, continuing past the glasshouses until you come onto a broad track where you turn right up to the road. To your left here, you will find a footpath sign pointing back diagonally over the field. The line of the path goes right across to the far right-hand corner but there is no sign of it on the ground and you will either have to walk through the crop or, if you quail at that, go round the edge to the left. At the far corner, turn into the next field and walk towards the pine plantation. When you come to a ride through the plantation, cross over the wire fence out of the field and take the broad track to your right, keeping the trees on your left. At the bottom of the hill, cross a small concrete bridge over the Mill river. There are springs to the left in the marshy ground. Note the sandy craggy hill behind with rabbit burrows. There is quite a lot of

WHEATEAR

BRIGHTWELL TO NEWBOURNE

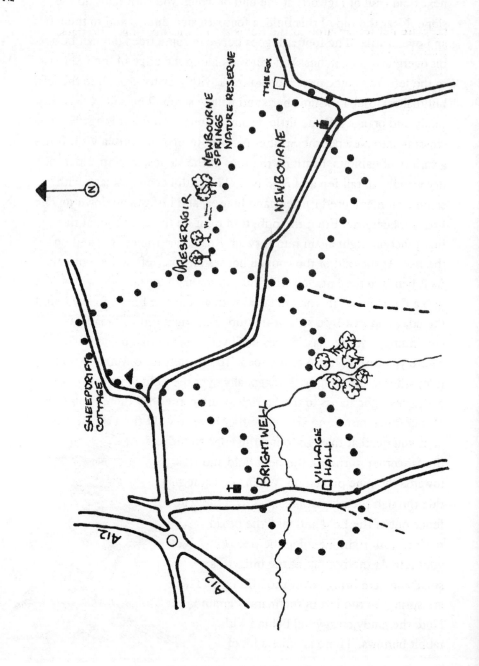

BRIGHTWELL TO NEWBOURNE